Listen-In'

Listening/Speaking Attack Strategies for Students of ESL

Burt Gabler
City College of San Francisco

Nadia F. Scholnick
City College of San Francisco

ST. MARTIN'S PRESS
NEW YORK

Editor: Naomi Silverman
Associate editor: Carl Whithaus
Managing editor: Patricia Mansfield Phelan
Project editor: Amy Horowitz
Production manager: Patricia Ollague
Text design: Sheree Goodman
Photo research: Inge King
Cover design: Rod Hernandez
Line art: Academy Artworks, Inc.
Audiotape producer: Paul Ruben Productions

Library of Congress Catalog Card Number: 94-65196

Manufactured in the United States of America.

9 8 7 6 5
f e d c b a

For information, write:
St. Martin's Press, Inc.
175 Fifth Avenue
New York, NY 10010

ISBN: 0-312-11110-X

In loving memory of
Dennis Martin
1946–1990

and
in honor of our parents

Sophie Gabler
Julian Gabler

Lynne Okon Scholnick
Joseph B. Scholnick

Overview

Listen-In' was developed for adult English as a Second Language (ESL) students in either academic or adult education programs. In addition to providing intensive listening skill training, *Listen-In'* offers extensive conversation and speaking practice through the use of a variety of learning techniques.

Central to *Listen-In'* is the understanding that teaching listening involves much more than simply supplying students with a listening encounter. Students must take a proactive stance vis-à-vis listening comprehension. To become good listeners, students need to use specific listening attack strategies and develop appropriate attitudes toward the listening process. In other words, students must learn how to listen. *Listen-In'* facilitates the acquisition of effective listening skills by creating a language laboratory in the classroom where trial and error and risk taking are encouraged through self-directed techniques that train students to develop an ongoing pattern of prediction, negotiation, and renegotiation.

Listening Attack Strategies

Listen-In' focuses on the use of eight specific listening attack strategies. They are:

Using What You Already Know

Scanning for Background Information

Scanning for the Main Idea

Inferencing (Making Intelligent Guesses)

Scanning for Specific Pieces of Information

Using Context Clues

Using Structure and Intonation Clues

Revising Assumptions (Checking What You Understood)

Listening comprehension is presented within a context of realistic and familiar topics. The content of the dialogues is relevant and is something to which students can relate their personal experiences. Students at the high-beginning or intermediate level of language learning have not yet developed the basic language skills necessary to successfully process materials heavily laden with unfamiliar information or subject matter. These low- to mid-level students, whether they are in an academic or nonacademic learning environment, are concerned with basic communication skills, both active and passive. They are not ready or able to tackle subjects outside their realm of experience *in addition to* developing basic language skills. By presenting listening comprehension training within a relevant and immediate context, *Listen-In'* meets the real needs and concerns of *all* students at this level of language acquisition.

Listen-In' also provides a framework through which increasingly complex information and culturally enriching knowledge are spiraled. Exercises and activities overlap, thus ensuring that past language encounters are reinforced while at the same time foreshadowing language that the student will later encounter.

Chapter Format

Except for Chapter One, all chapters have the same format.

Part I
Pre-listening

Pre-listening activities anticipate the language that will be heard in the sample dialogues. Rather than have information spoonfed by the instructor, students are divided into small groups and asked to pool information and clarify any misunderstandings within the framework of a support unit. By the time the listening activity begins, students have retrieved a great amount of the information they already possess and will be ready to match their concepts of the issues and attitudes discussed in the situation at hand with those of the speakers.

Part II
Main Dialogue

The goals of the exercises in Part II are clearly identified at the beginning of each task and are geared alternately toward extracting small pieces of specific information or toward gleaning general information; they are *never* geared toward total comprehension or recall. To help teach students how to use listening attack strategies, the main dialogue must be long enough so that students *cannot* understand everything on the first listening. Students are compensated by the fact that by the end of the unit they will have acquired a sufficient understanding of the material to make sense of the discourse studied.

Exercise 1 begins with the first sampling of the main dialogue. For the first sampling, students are asked to consider basic information related to the wants, needs, and backgrounds of the speakers. Here, students are encouraged to predict how nonlinguistic elements of communication contribute to comprehension.

In Exercise 2, students are asked to begin negotiating the major issues of the dialogue through the assistance of structured questions. Discussion of the questions and answers allows students to share the information they gleaned as well as their individual methods of arriving at assumptions. The instructor acts as facilitator in this process by reinforcing the notion that there are not necessarily right and wrong answers. Rather, *all* answers are encouraged because they provide the means, via renegotiation, by which listening comprehension is ultimately reached. Here, as in many other places in the book, students should share how they utilized various bits of information to arrive at correct assumptions.

After arriving at a general understanding of the main dialogue, students are asked, in Exercise 3, to listen to the dialogue one more time, but this time only for discrete pieces of information. Here, students are taught to focus their attention on specific aspects of the dialogue and to learn how to filter out extraneous information.

Exercise 4 provides closure and ensures that all students are satisfied with their understanding of the materials. To aid students in refining their understanding of some of the more difficult utterances in the conversation, specific words and phrases are highlighted and students are asked to negotiate meaning by using context clues.

In some chapters, a fifth exercise is added to extend the discussion of that chapter's topic.

Part III
Expansion

This section of the chapter focuses on topics introduced in the main dialogue. Expansion exercises make use of short readings, maps, diagrams, and so on as suggested by the chapter theme. Students are given an opportunity to develop a deeper understanding of relevant topics through group discovery. Additionally, Expansion activities allow students to utilize listening attack strategies through a less controlled approach.

Part IV
Focus

Focus begins with an examination of how various discrete points of grammar, syntax, or aspects of the suprasegmentals of English can be exploited to further aid in listening comprehension. This portion of the chapter is not meant to introduce new structures. Rather, students are taught to utilize their pre-existing knowledge of grammar, syntax, stress, pitch, and intonation as an additional tool to decipher unknown language. Students are shown that, despite difficulties with vocabulary, speed of speech, or other perceived impediments to comprehension, a great deal of meaning can be gleaned through exploiting the clues provided by specific points of grammar, syntax, and suprasegmentals.

Part V
Listening Practice

The Listening Practice section of each chapter has four exercises designed to reinforce all of the strategies, techniques, and topics previously encountered. Although the format of the exercises varies in Chapter 5, the exercises in the rest of the chapters follow a consistent format. In the first exercise, students are asked to choose appropriate responses to questions that they hear. In the second, students are asked to select sentences that are correct based on the meaning of what they hear. In the third, short dialogues are presented in which information changes during the course of the conversation. Here, students must use the strategy of revising assumptions. In the fourth, several dialogues, each preceded by a question, are presented. This exercise requires that students make inferences based on information contained in the dialogues. This section of the chapter should be presented in a listening lab format. The exercises are not intended to serve as chapter tests. Like other exercises in the text, the Listening Practice exercises do not all have strict right or wrong answers. Rather, it is important that teachers help students identify the specific strategies they utilized to arrive at their responses.

Part VI
Using It

In the final section of each chapter, a highly de-controlled exercise is presented. Students are asked to work cooperatively on a variety of projects which are product-oriented. Through the use of persuasion, negotiation, and compromise, students learn to synthesize their skills both linguistically and creatively. Typically, in this section students will develop role plays for class presentation, complete contact assignments in which they must interact in real settings with native speakers, and/or complete problem solving and conceptual tasks. In all cases, students are responsible for both gathering and presenting information to their classmates.

Group Work

Listen-In' is structured so that many activities are group oriented. Working in pairs or small groups gives students a more active approach to learning. Cooperative learning also encourages students to take responsibility for their learning experience. The tasks in *Listen-In'* require that students compare, contrast, and pool their knowledge and relevant experiences to gain necessary information while the instructor functions as facilitator.

Icons

Tape icons are placed throughout the text to indicate those portions of each chapter that are presented on tape. Similarly, vocal tabs are placed on the audiotapes so that instructors can progress through each lesson easily and efficiently. Note that the instructor will need to rewind the tape for those exercises requiring a second or third playing (for example, exercises in Part II's Main Dialogue).

Audiotapes

A set of five audiotapes accompanies this text. Please contact your college bookstore to order them.

To maximize student involvement with the learning and practice of listening attack strategies and to ensure that students are not tempted to rely on rote memorization of dialogues, tape scripts are not included in this text.

Instructor's Manual

This text is accompanied by an Instructor's Manual that offers suggested answers and follow-up exercises.

About the Title

Listen-In' represents three distinct and equally important meanings. First, the title suggests that the listening process is self-directed, focused, and purposeful. Students need to "listen in" to become better listeners. Second, spoken English is laden with numerous reduced forms. Students need to learn how to recognize and identify reductions, contractions, and other potential impediments to comprehension. "Listenin'" to English is not always easy! Finally, borrowing from the 1960s' Love-Ins, Be-Ins, and Teach-Ins we enjoyed in our youth, we offer *Listen-In'* as an opportunity for teachers and students to experience mutually beneficial growth and development through discovery and exploration. Welcome to our *Listen-In'*!

Acknowledgments

Many talented individuals have assisted in the development of this textbook.

VOICES ON FIELD-TEST TAPES

Reenie Haughey
Bob Leydorf
Lenni Terao
Doug Doerr
Dennis Martin
Steve Teresi
Travis Amos
Barbara Stewart
Sophie Gabler
Susan Heis
Bill Russell

INITIAL ARTWORK

Reiko Goto
Tim Collins

FIELD TESTERS

Joy Durigello
Annie Wong
Carole Glanzer
Ed Murray
Kim Lee
Robin Mollica
Nina Gibson

ADVICE AND SUGGESTIONS

Joanne Low
Kathleen Wong
Elsa Rael
Eric "MBTL" Scholnick

Thanks to the St. Martin's Press reviewers: Bonnie Cothren, Pacific Lutheran University; Sally C. Gearheart, Santa Rosa Junior College; Linda Reingardt, University of Pittsburgh and Guinn Roberts, Educational Testing Service, Princeton, New Jersey. We also thank our wonderfully insightful editor Naomi Silverman, our associate editor Carl Whithaus, our project editor Amy Horowitz, and our tape producer Paul Ruben.

Thanks go as well to our families, friends, and neighbors for providing the inspiration for many of the dialogues.

Finally, a big thank you to our friends, colleagues, and students at City College of San Francisco for their support and encouragement. We would especially like to thank Karen Saginor for assistance with the library materials and Marge Ryder and Linda Schurer for their invaluable help with editing the Focus sections.

Burt Gabler
Nadia F. Scholnick

CONTENTS

Chapter Four _____
Medical Needs and Services: "A Healthy Excuse"   43

Chapter Five _____
Shopping: "Which One Is the Better Buy?"   57

Chapter Six _____
Community Services: "A Tight Balancing Act"   71

CHAPTER ONE

Learning to Listen

Part I   **Preparing for the Listening Encounter: Questionnaire**

Directions: Form groups of three or four students. Make sure that your group does not have students who all speak the same native language. Decide whether each of the following statements is *True* or *False*.

1. When you are listening to English, it isn't necessary to first know something about the topic.

2. When you are listening to an English conversation, it isn't necessary to think about who and where the speakers are: Just listen to their words.

3. When you are listening to English, you must understand 100 percent of the words to understand the main idea.

4. When you are listening to English, you can only get information from what people say (the exact words they use).

5. When you are listening to English and need to know a specific piece of information, you need to pay careful attention to every word.

6. When you are listening to English, you should find out the meaning of every word that you don't understand.

7. Your knowledge of grammar and intonation can only help you with writing and speaking, not with listening.

8. After you correctly understand information in a conversation, you can relax and do not need to think about that information anymore.

Now that you have discussed the eight statements with your classmates and teacher, you have figured out that all eight statements are false. If you do what these eight statements suggest, your listening comprehension will *not* improve.

To be a good listener, you need to use *listening attack strategies*. A *strategy* is a special kind of plan. For example, if you want your boss to give you a raise, you need to make a specific plan about how to talk to him or her about it. You need to tell your boss why you deserve the raise. You also should think about what he or she might say to you so that you can prepare good answers. To be successful, you need to have a good attack strategy.

To improve your listening comprehension, you also need to use good attack strategies. In this book you will learn about the following eight listening attack strategies:

1. Using What You Already Know
2. Scanning for Background Information
3. Scanning for the Main Idea
4. Inferencing (Making Intelligent Guesses)
5. Scanning for Specific Pieces of Information
6. Using Context Clues
7. Using Structure and Intonation Clues
8. Revising Assumptions (Checking What You Understood)

Now, take a few minutes to discuss what you think each of these listening attack strategies means. Part II will give you more information about each strategy and show you how each strategy works.

Part II   Listening Attack Strategies

1. _____
Using What You Already Know

It is very important to use all of the information that you already have about a topic when you listen to English. This will help you prepare for what you may hear. For example, if you know that you will visit your school counselor, you should first think about the kinds of things you will probably discuss. Let's prepare a list of some of the words that you might hear when you talk to your counselor. Add to the list that has already been started.

PROGRAM	LEVEL	PLACEMENT	APPOINTMENT	APPLICATION
_____	_____	_____	_____	_____
_____	_____	_____	_____	_____

P R A C T I C E

Exercise 1

Directions: Listen to a short conversation between a student and counselor. Circle all of the words in the list that you hear.

You probably circled many of the words in the list because these are common words for this situation. Notice how much easier it is to understand when you already have an idea about what the topic is.

Exercise 2   **Directions:** Pretend that you walk into the school library and sit down across from the two people in the photograph. Before listening to their conversation, try to guess what they are talking about and write your guess on the line below.

_____

Now, listen to what they say.

Did you guess correctly? Using what you already know about the world is an important listening attack strategy.

2. _____
Scanning For Background Information

To become a better listener, you also need to think about who and where the speakers are. The way the speakers look and sound can help you to understand what they are saying even if you do not understand all of their words. It is helpful to try to guess as much information as you can about the people you are listening to. Listen to the following example.

From the speaker's tone of voice, we can guess that she is very angry. Because her language is formal, we can make a good guess that she probably doesn't know the person she is speaking with very well. Finally, we hear the word "registration" which tells us that maybe the speaker is at a school, a motor vehicle department, or similar place.

Thinking about who and where the speakers are, how they sound, and what they might want or need can help your listening comprehension.

Directions: Listen to the following speakers, and then circle the words that you feel *might* be true about them.

1. excited / upset

   formal / informal

   librarian / student

   school / restaurant / office

   young / middle-aged / old

2. restaurant / department store

   polite / impolite

   young / middle-aged / old

   foreigner / native speaker

   confident / shy

3. department store / bookstore / registration office

   young / middle-aged / old

   annoyed / confused / concerned

4. Place: library / hospital / cafeteria / classroom

   Woman: young / middle-aged / old

             excited / angry

             high / mid / low level of education

   Man: young / middle-aged / old

             patient / impatient

             high / mid / low level of education

5. Place: student health center / testing office / work place

   Man: young / middle-aged / old

             student / teacher

             angry / worried / patient

             rich / not rich

   Woman: young / middle-aged / old

             professional / unprofessional

             doctor / teacher / student / receptionist

You probably noticed that there were no right or wrong answers in this exercise. **Scanning for background information** is just a way of helping you form a picture of who and where the speakers are and what they want or are doing. Your first guesses might turn out to be wrong, but that's okay. Later on, when you hear more of the conversation and get more information, you can change your ideas if you need to. The important thing is that this listening attack strategy can get you started.

3.
Scanning for the Main Idea

Good listeners do not worry about the meaning of every word or phrase they hear. They concentrate on trying to understand the speaker's ideas. When you are listening to speech in your native language, you can not always understand every word that is spoken. But, you usually have no problem getting the main idea. You need to use this same listening attack strategy in English.

P R A C T I C E

Directions: Listen to the following conversation to find the main idea. The two speakers have a problem. What is it? In the blank spaces, write down the main idea and any words that help you guess what the problem is.

Main Idea: _____

Key Words

  Food machines   _____   _____

  _____   _____   _____

4.
Inferencing (Making Intelligent Guesses)

Good listeners know that a lot of meaning is understood from the situation, the needs of the speakers and what is and is not said.

Let's take a look at an example. Pretend that you see your teacher after class and that you want to discuss your homework. As you are talking you see that your teacher keeps looking at his watch. What can you infer from this?

Here's another example. You are sitting in class and there is an empty seat next to you. A student comes in and asks you, "Is anybody sitting here?" What is this student really asking you?

In both examples, the speakers did not say exactly what they mean, but you were still able to understand their meaning.

Directions: Listen to the following conversation, and circle the answers that you feel are true. Then, discuss with your teacher how you used inferencing to decide.

1. Ted needs some help with his school work.
2. Ted is doing very well in Dr. Stevens's class.
3. Ted doesn't really want to meet with Dr. Stevens.
4. Ted is serious about his school work.
5. Dr. Stevens is interested in helping his students.

5. _____
Scanning for Specific Pieces of Information

Sometimes it is necessary to listen for specific pieces of information (times, dates, names, places, and so on). In these situations, you need to learn how to organize the information that you hear. You have to pay attention only to the specific pieces of information you need and not worry about anything else.

Directions: Listen to the following recorded message, and fill in the chart with the specific information needed.

Student Union Activity Hotline

Place	Activity	Time	Price
cafeteria		7:00-8:30 AM	X
	lunch		X
cafeteria	dinner		X
snack bar	X		diverse
Oak Room		9:00-10:00 AM	
		noon-1:30 PM	free
	Folk Dance Club		free
Campus Cabaret	Bette Milder		
	"Dial Tones"	7:00/9:00 PM	

6. _____
Using Context Clues

Understanding the meaning of what you hear is more important than understanding all of the vocabulary words that you hear. Sometimes you will hear words that you don't know, but you can still figure out the meaning because you know what the speakers are talking about. The words and even the sentences around the new words help you to understand the meaning.

Listen to this conversation that contains vocabulary words you do not know.

You may not have understood the sentence, "Wait a second, this pen just died." However, by focusing on the context around the sentence, it's easy to make a good guess. Let's listen to the sentence and its context again.

Does "Wait a second, this pen just died" mean:

1. I can't write: my pen doesn't work.

or

2. I can't write: my hand hurts.

Of course the correct answer is (1) "I can't write: my pen doesn't work."

You were able to figure out the answer from the context. The words, "Here, take my pencil," tell you that the speaker's pen is not working. Using the context will help you understand meaning and is a very important way to help you improve your listening skills.

P R A C T I C E

Directions: You will hear five short dialogues. Each dialogue will contain a sentence with vocabulary words you may not know. After you hear the sentence a second time, circle the answer with the same meaning.

1. **(a)** He's very strict.

(b) He's very interesting.

2. **(a)** I was really happy.

(b) I was really surprised.

3. **(a)** I am late for a test.

(b) I have to study for a test.

4. **(a)** We should relax for a while.

(b) We need to begin right now.

5. **(a)** I don't think that's possible.

(b) I think that's possible.

7.
Using Structure and Intonation Clues

Your knowledge of structure (grammar and word order) and intonation will help you improve your listening comprehension. Structure and intonation can give you clues even when you don't understand all of the vocabulary. You need to learn how to use what you already know about structure and intonation to help you improve your listening skills.

For example, you already know that the present progressive tense in English can show two different times: It can show actions that are occurring right now or actions that will occur in the future. You have also learned that when we use the present progressive tense to mean future time, we use a time word (such as *tomorrow*, *next week*, *at 3:00*) to show the future. Every time you hear the present progressive tense, you know that you need to listen for the time word to understand when the time of the action is taking place.

PRACTICE

Here are three short exercises to help you practice identifying the proper time.

Exercise 1

Directions: Listen to the following sentences. Decide whether each indicates *present* or *future* time. Circle the answer.

1. **(a)** Present   **(b)** Future

2. **(a)** Present   **(b)** Future

3. **(a)** Present   **(b)** Future

4. **(a)** Present   **(b)** Future

5. **(a)** Present   **(b)** Future

Exercise 2

Directions: Listen to the following sentences, and circle the sentence that has the same meaning.

1. **(a)** I'm working now.

   (b) I will work later.

2. **(a)** It is happening now.

   (b) It will happen later.

3. **(a)** We're doing it now.

   (b) We will do it in the future.

4. **(a)** I'm doing it now.

   (b) I will do it in the future.

5. **(a)** She is doing it now.

   (b) She will do it in the future.

Exercise 3   **Directions:** Listen to the following sentences. Then, circle the sentence that best follows.

1. (a) Let's be quiet.

    (b) We can study for a few more minutes.

2. (a) Let's be quiet.

    (b) We can study for a few more minutes.

3. (a) Too bad! I'll be out of town.

    (b) If we hurry, we can see the second half of the play.

4. (a) Too bad! I'll be out of town.

    (b) If we hurry, we can see the second half of the play.

5. (a) Let's go buy a few.

    (b) Good! I'll get my check before then.

6. (a) Let's go buy a few.

    (b) Good! I'll get my check before then.

8.
Revising Assumptions (Checking What You Understood)

When people have conversations, they are usually thinking while they are talking. Because of this, people change their minds about things they have already said. Sometimes information that is true at the beginning of a conversation is very different by the end of the conversation. To be a good listener, you have to be ready for these changes. You need to practice checking what you understand with changes in the conversation.

P R A C T I C E

Directions: Listen to the following conversation. Each time you hear the bell, circle the sentence that you think is correct. Discuss each answer with your instructor.

1. **(a)** The person did something illegal.

   (b) The person did not do something illegal.

2. **(a)** The person did something illegal.

   (b) The person did not do something illegal.

3. **(a)** The person will have to pay more insurance.

   (b) The person will not have to pay more insurance.

4. **(a)** The person will have to pay more insurance.

   (b) The person will not have to pay more insurance.

5. **(a)** The person will have to pay the fine for the parking ticket.

   (b) The person will not have to pay the fine for the parking ticket.

6. **(a)** The person will pay the fine.

   (b) The person will not pay the fine.

   (c) The person might pay the fine.

If you changed your answers as you heard more information in the conversation, you were correctly revising your assumptions. This is an important listening attack strategy.

In this book, you will practice using all of the listening attack strategies you have just learned about. When you do the exercises in this book, you should always discuss with your classmates and teacher how you decide on the answers you choose. If you make mistakes, you shouldn't feel bad. You should talk about the listening attack strategies that you used, and find out from other students which strategies they used to get the correct answers.

Sometimes you will notice that more than one answer is correct. Language is not always clear and sometimes more than one meaning is possible. When this happens, you should use your understanding of the listening attack strategies to discuss why different answers may work.

Part III   Using It: Talking about Talking

Directions: In pairs or small groups, try to think of attack strategies that can be used for speaking. After your group has made a list of speaking attack strategies, get together with your classmates and teacher to share your answers.

To help you with your list, think about the following questions.

1. Do you have to use perfect grammar or pronunciation when you speak?

2. Is it a good idea to think about what you are going to say in your native language first?

3. Should you use a dictionary when you are speaking English?

4. Should you wait until your English is perfect before you try speaking with people you don't know?

5. Is it impolite to use body language when you speak English?

Write down as many strategies as you can think of. The first one has been filled in for you.

SPEAKING ATTACK STRATEGIES

1. When you are speaking English, you should not translate word-for-word from your native language.

2. _____

3. _____

4. _____

5. _____

6. _____

7. _____

Transportation: "Just the Directions, Please"

Part I   Pre-listening: Map Exercise

The San Francisco Bay area has a transportation system (the Bay Area Rapid Transit system or BART) that connects thirty-four stations in an area that stretches from Daly City to Concord and from the city of Richmond to the city of Fremont (see BART Line Map on page 14). BART is one of the most modern metros in the world. The trains are operated by computers and even the electronically coded tickets are sold through computerized machines. BART station platforms have electronic signs that light up with information about trains that will be arriving.

Exercise 1   **Directions:** Look at the BART Line Map. Divide into pairs or small groups and answer the following questions.

1. How many different lines are there in the BART system? What are their names?
2. Do all lines go to San Francisco? If not, explain.
3. How many stations are there in San Francisco?
4. How many lines go to Berkeley? What are they?
5. How many lines go to Fruitvale? What are they?
6. How many lines go to Rockridge? What are they?
7. Look at the Concord/Daly City line. Is the symbol for the Concord/Daly City line marked by a white line, a black line, a line with dots, or a line with Xs? How many stations are there on the Concord/Daly City line?
8. Find South Hayward on the map. Can you go to South Hayward on the Concord line? If not, what would you do if you were on a Concord train coming from San Francisco and you wanted to go to South Hayward?
9. Can you go directly from San Leandro to Walnut Creek? If not, how can you go from San Leandro to Walnut Creek? In which direction will your first train be going?
10. How many BART stations have parking lots?
11. Which stations are the most important for transferring from one BART line to a different BART line?

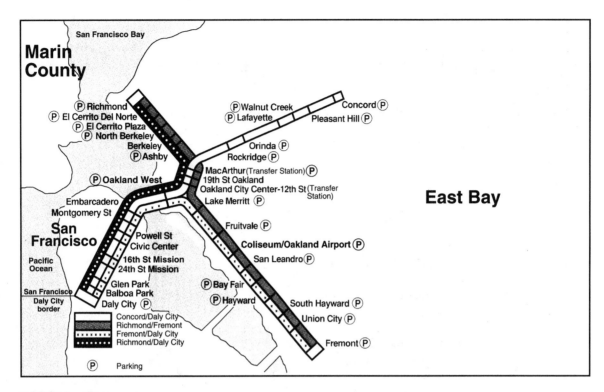

BART Line Map

Part II Main Dialogue

Exercise 1

Directions: Listen to the dialogue and try to get a general idea of what is happening. It may help to look at the BART map while you listen to the dialogue. Remember, you don't need to understand everything. Just try to think about the following questions:

- Where do you think this dialogue is taking place?
- Who are the people in the dialogue?
- About how old do you think the speakers are?
- Do the speakers sound happy, angry, sad, friendly, unfriendly, sarcastic, annoyed, patient, impatient, and so on?

Exercise 2

rewind

Directions: Now listen to the dialogue again to answer these questions:

1. Who are Denise and Tom going to visit?
2. What famous place is near their destination?
3. How does the young woman find out the price of their BART ticket?
4. Why are there different BART ticket prices?
5. How do Denise and Tom feel about the young woman? Why?
6. How does the young woman feel about Denise and Tom? Why?
7. What does the title "Just the Directions, Please" mean?

Exercise 3

rewind

Directions: Listen to the dialogue one more time. Then, fill in the chart with information as you hear it.

Time of dialogue	
Tom and Denise's destination	
Station where dialogue takes place	
Ticket price to destination	

Trip Schedule

First Train	
Name of line	
Departure time	
Transfer station	
Arrival time at transfer station	

Second Train	
Name of Line	
Departure time	
Time of arrival at destination	

Exercise 4

Directions: Listen to these sentences from the dialogue, and circle the answer that has the same meaning.

1. **(a)** Her house is near the university.

   (b) Her house is the stone house near the university.

2. **(a)** How long is the trip to downtown Berkeley?

   (b) What is the price to downtown Berkeley?

3. **(a)** That's a dangerous trip.

   (b) That's an expensive trip.

4. **(a)** You don't have to get off the Richmond train to go to Berkeley.

   (b) It doesn't take long on the Richmond train to get to Berkeley.

(Continued)

5. **(a)** It will be easy to make the trip.

(b) It will be enjoyable to make the trip.

6. **(a)** I think you are single.

(b) I think you don't like rings.

Part III   Expansion: Charts and Schedules

Exercise 1   **Directions:** Divide into pairs or small groups to answer the following questions. Look at the BART Time and Fares Chart on page 17. *Note: Time* refers to the length of time (the duration of the trip) from one station to another. It does not refer to arrival and departure times.

1. How much does it cost to go from 16th Street Mission to San Leandro?
2. How much is a round-trip ticket between Balboa Park and El Cerrito Plaza?
3. How long does it take to go from Daly City to Montgomery Street?
4. How many minutes does it take to go from Powell Street to Rockridge?
5. What is the most expensive trip in the BART system? What is the longest trip in the BART system?

Now, look on page 18 at the two schedules for the Metro-North Commuter Railroad service between Grand Central Terminal and Yonkers, New York.

1. What does *G.C.T.* mean?
2. Which schedule would you look at if you wanted to go to Marble Hill from G.C.T.?
3. Which schedule would you look at if you wanted to go to University Heights from Yonkers?
4. What time does the next train from G.C.T. going to Yonkers leave? What time will it arrive? (Look at your watch or a clock and use the current time to answer this question.)
5. Which stations does the 8:04 AM train from Yonkers to G.C.T. stop at?
6. If you want to arrive in Ludlow by 8:30 PM, which train should you take from G.C.T.?
7. Can you get train service between G.C.T. and Yonkers twenty-four hours a day, Monday through Friday?
8. What do you think the shaded areas on the schedule show?

Fares

These fares are subject to change. Please verify prior to ticket purchase.

This is the BART Time and Fares Chart — a triangular distance/fare matrix. The upper-right triangle gives fares (in dollars) and the lower-left triangle gives travel times (in minutes) between pairs of stations. The stations, listed along the diagonal, are:

Daly City, Balboa Park, Glen Park, 24th St. Mission, 16th St. Mission, Civic Center, Powell, Montgomery, Embarcadero, Oakland West, Concord, Pleasant Hill, Walnut Creek, Lafayette, Orinda, Rockridge, Richmond, El Cerrito Del Norte, El Cerrito Plaza, North Berkeley, Berkeley, Ashby, MacArthur, 19th St. Oakland, Oak. City Cnr. 12th St., Lake Merritt, Fruitvale, Coliseum, San Leandro, Bay Fair, Hayward, South Hayward, Union City, Fremont.

BART Time and Fares Chart

TO GRAND CENTRAL TERMINAL, NEW YORK

MONDAY TO FRIDAY, EXCEPT HOLIDAYS

Leave Yonkers	Ludlow	Riverdale W. 254 St.	Spuyten Duyvil	Marble Hill W. 225 St.	Univ. Heights W. 207 St.	Morris Heights W. 177 St.	125 St.	Arrive G.C.T.
AM	AM	AM	AM	AM	AM	AM	AM	AM
12:17	12:19	12:22	12:25	12:27	12:30	12:32	‡12:39	12:50
T 5:32	T 5:34	T 5:37	T 5:40	T 5:42	......	......	T 5:51	6:02
6:02	6:04	6:07	6:10	6:12	......	......	6:21	6:32
6:27	6:29	6:32	6:35	6:37	6:40	6:42	6:48	7:00
7:01	7:03	7:06	7:09	7:11	7:14	7:16	7:22	7:35
X 7:22	X 7:24	X 7:27	X 7:31	X 7:33	......	......	......	7:53
7:38	7:41	7:44	7:50	7:52	7:55	7:57	8:04	8:17
XT 7:52	XT 7:55	XT 7:58	......	......	......	......	......	8:23
8:04	......	......	8:13	8:15	8:18	8:20	8:26	8:39
8:18	8:21	8:24	8:28	8:30	......	......	D 8:38	8:51
8:35	8:37	8:40	8:44	8:46	8:49	8:51	8:58	9:11
9:17	9:19	9:22	9:25	9:27	9:30	9:32	9:38	9:50
9:42	9:44	9:47	9:50	9:52	......	......	‡10:01	10:12
10:07	10:09	10:12	10:15	10:17	10:20	10:22	‡10:29	10:40
11:07	11:09	11:12	11:15	11:17	11:20	11:22	‡11:29	11:40
12:07	12:09	12:12	12:15	12:17	12:20	12:22	‡12:29	12:40
1:07	1:09	1:12	1:15	1:17	1:20	1:22	‡ 1:29	1:40
2:07	2:09	2:12	2:15	2:17	2:20	2:22	‡ 2:29	2:40
3:07	3:09	3:12	3:15	3:17	3:20	3:22	‡ 3:29	3:40
3:37	......	......	......	3:44	......	......	‡ 3:56	4:07
4:07	4:09	4:12	4:15	4:17	4:20	4:22	‡ 4:29	4:41
4:37	......	......	......	4:44	......	......	‡ 4:56	5:09
5:07	5:09	5:12	5:15	5:17	5:20	5:22	‡ 5:29	5:41
5:37	......	......	......	5:44	......	......	‡ 5:56	6:09
6:02	6:04	6:07	6:10	6:12	6:15	6:17	‡ 6:24	6:35
7:07	7:09	7:12	7:15	7:17	7:20	7:22	‡ 7:29	7:40
8:07	8:09	8:12	8:15	8:17	8:20	8:22	‡ 8:29	8:40
9:07	9:09	9:12	9:15	9:17	......	......	‡ 9:27	9:38
10:07	10:09	10:12	10:15	10:17	......	......	‡10:27	10:38
11:02	11:04	11:07	11:10	11:12	11:15	11:17	‡11:24	11:35
12:17	12:19	12:22	12:25	12:27	12:30	12:32	‡12:39	12:50
AM	AM	AM	AM	AM	AM	AM	AM	AM

FROM GRAND CENTRAL TERMINAL, NEW YORK

MONDAY TO FRIDAY, EXCEPT HOLIDAYS

Leave G.C.T.	125 St.	Morris Heights W. 177 St.	Univ. Heights W. 207 St.	Marble Hill W. 225 St.	Spuyten Duyvil	Riverdale W. 254 St.	Ludlow	Arrive Yonkers
AM	AM	AM	AM	AM	AM	AM	AM	AM
12:20	12:31	12:37	12:39	12:42	12:44	12:47	12:50	12:52
1:20	1:31	1:37	1:39	1:42	1:44	1:47	1:50	1:52
6:20	6:31	6:37	6:39	6:42	6:44	6:47	6:50	6:52
7:20	7:31	7:37	7:39	7:42	7:44	7:47	7:50	7:52
T 7:48	R 7:59	......	......	8:07	......	......	......	8:16
8:20	8:31	8:37	8:39	8:42	8:44	8:47	8:50	8:52
9:20	9:31	9:37	9:39	9:42	9:44	9:47	9:50	9:52
10:20	10:31	10:37	10:39	10:42	10:44	10:47	10:50	10:52
11:20	11:31	11:37	11:39	11:42	11:44	11:47	11:50	11:52
12:20	12:31	12:37	12:39	12:42	12:44	12:47	12:50	12:52
1:20	1:31	1:37	1:39	1:42	1:44	1:47	1:50	1:52
2:20	2:31	2:37	2:39	2:42	2:44	2:47	2:50	2:52
3:20	3:31	3:37	3:39	3:42	3:44	3:47	3:50	3:52
3:50	4:01	4:07	4:09	4:12	4:14	4:17	4:20	4:22
4:20	4:31	......	......	4:39	4:41	4:44	4:47	4:49
4:53	5:04	5:10	5:12	5:15	5:18	5:21	5:24	5:27
5:14	R 5:25	......	......	5:33	5:36	5:39	5:42	5:45
T 5:37	5:48	5:55	5:57	6:00	6:03	6:06	6:09	6:12
5:59	6:10	6:16	6:18	6:21	6:24	6:27	6:30	6:33
6:20	6:31	6:37	6:39	6:42	6:44	6:47	6:50	6:52
6:55	7:06	7:12	7:14	7:17	7:19	7:22	7:25	7:27
7:20	7:31	7:37	7:39	7:42	7:44	7:47	7:50	7:52
7:53	8:04	......	......	8:12	8:14	8:17	8:20	8:22
8:20	8:31	8:37	8:39	8:42	8:44	8:47	8:50	8:52
9:20	9:31	9:37	9:39	9:42	9:44	9:47	9:50	9:52
10:20	10:31	10:37	10:39	10:42	10:44	10:47	10:50	10:52
11:20	11:31	11:37	11:39	11:42	11:44	11:47	11:50	11:52
12:20	12:31	12:37	12:39	12:42	12:44	12:47	12:50	12:52
1:20	1:31	1:37	1:39	1:42	1:44	1:47	1:50	1:52
AM	AM	AM	AM	AM	AM	AM	AM	AM

Metro-North Commuter Railroad Schedules

Exercise 2

Directions: Divide into pairs and decide who will be partner A and who will be partner B. Then, ask and answer the following questions.

Partner A: First, ask your partner the following questions and write down the answers he or she gives you. Do *not* look at the BART Times and Fares Chart!

Second, after you are finished writing the answers, look at the Metro-North Commuter Railroad schedules for service between Grand Central Terminal and Yonkers. Use the schedules to answer your partner's questions. Do *not* let your partner see the schedules!

1. How much does it cost to go from Civic Center to Oakland West?
2. What is the fare from Embarcadero to North Berkeley?
3. How long does it take to go from 16th Street Mission to Civic Center?
4. How many minutes is it from Montgomery Street to 12th Street Oakland?
5. How much is a round-trip ticket from Powell Street to Fremont?

Partner B: First, look at the BART Times and Fares Chart and answer your partner's questions. Do *not* let your partner see the chart.

Second, after your partner is finished writing the answers, ask your partner the following questions and write the answers that he or she gives you. Do *not* look at the schedules!

1. Look at your watch or a clock. What time does the next train to West 177th Street from Yonkers leave?
2. How many stops are there from Yonkers to Grand Central Terminal?
3. What time does the first afternoon train from Yonkers to Grand Central Terminal leave?
4. How many trains go from Grand Central Terminal to Yonkers from 12 P.M. until 3:50 P.M.?
5. What time does the 12:20 A.M. train from Grand Central Terminal arrive in Yonkers?

Exercise 3   **Directions:** For questions 1–6, look at the BART Times and Fares Chart and answer the questions using information from the chart. To help organize the information you hear, you will need to take notes. It may be helpful to use symbols. For example, if you need to know the time, use the symbol *T*. If you need to know the price, use the symbol for dollar sign, *$*.

1. _____

2. _____

3. _____

4. _____

5. _____

6. _____

Directions: For questions 7–10, look at the schedules for the New York Metro-North Commuter Railroad service between Grand Central Terminal and Yonkers, and answer the questions using the information from the schedules. Again, use any symbols that will help you organize the information that you need to know.

7. _____

8. _____

9. _____

10. _____

Part IV   Focus: Yes/No and Information Questions

Listen to these sentences from the dialogue:

Do you think we'll make it in time?

Is there another train we can catch?

These are examples of *yes/no questions.* When someone asks a yes/no question, the intonation rises. Yes/no questions can be answered with a simple *yes* or *no*.

Listen to these sentences from the dialogue:

How much does it cost to ride BART?

What time is it?

These are examples of *information questions*. Information questions cannot be answered with a simple *yes* or *no*. Information questions have the same intonation as statements (falling intonation) and begin with question words such as *where*, *when*, *which*, *what*, *how*, *why*, and *who*. Information questions require the listener to provide some sort of information.

Wh–/Information Questions

The *wh–* word at the beginning of an information question shows the type of information the speaker wants you to give. If you do not understand the complete question the speaker asks, the *wh–* word you hear will give you an idea about what the speaker wants to know. For example, if the speaker does not know the place, he or she uses the *wh–* word *where*, which means *tell me the place*.

Wʜ– Wᴏʀᴅs ᴀɴᴅ Tʜᴇɪʀ Mᴇᴀɴɪɴɢs

where = place	*Where* is the nearest BART station?
who = people	*Who* lives in San Francisco?
what = information	*What* did you do yesterday?
when = time	*When* did you arrive in this country?
why = reason	*Why* were you so late?
whose = possession	*Whose* subway ticket is this?
which = choice of things	*Which* train should we take?
how often = frequency	*How often* do you take the train to work?
how far = distance	*How far* is it to Berkeley from here?
how long = length of time	*How long* does it take to get to Fremont?

Exercise 1

Directions: Repeat the following questions. Then, decide whether each is a yes/no question or an information question. Circle your answer.

1. Yes/no question
   Information question

2. Yes/no question
   Information question

3. Yes/no question
   Information question

4. Yes/no question
   Information question

5. Yes/no question
   Information question

6. Yes/no question
   Information question

7. Yes/no question
   Information question

8. Yes/no question
   Information question

9. Yes/no question
   Information question

10. Yes/no question
    Information question

In some situations, it is not always possible to clearly hear what the speaker is saying. If the room is noisy or there is a bad telephone connection, all of the words in a sentence may not be clear. However, if you pay close attention to intonation and *wh–* words, you can often figure out what information the speaker wants. In the following questions, some words will be difficult or impossible to hear. After you hear each question, decide which response is the best choice. Circle the correct answer.

Example   (a)   At 3:30.

         (b)   On the corner.

1.   (a) At the airport.

    (b) About an hour ago.

2.   (a) Once a week.

    (b) Yes, I went yesterday.

3.   (a) No, they had to take the bus home.

    (b) Their flight was very late.

4.   (a) No, she wasn't very late.

    (b) Because she couldn't find a phone.

5.   (a) My brother, Eric.

    (b) You can take the 5:00 train.

6.   (a) Because I didn't have time.

    (b) No, but my cousin was.

7.   (a) Yes, it's very far.

    (b) About ten miles.

8.   (a) The Number 49 Express.

    (b) At the downtown station.

9.   (a) No, it's not mine.

    (b) The old woman wearing a hat.

10.   (a) It takes forty-five minutes.

    (b) Yes, if I have time.

Exercise 3

Directions: Listen to the questions again. Write down what you think each question might be. (*Note:* there are many possibilities for each question.)

Part V   Listening Practice

Exercise 1

Directions: You will hear eight questions. Read the three possible responses and circle the correct answer.

1. (a) At 2:15.

    (b) 27 minutes.

    (c) $1.45.

2. (a) In five minutes.

    (b) Every ten minutes.

    (c) Yes, it's a Yonkers train.

3. (a) Yes, it does.

    (b) In ten minutes.

    (c) Take the number 32 bus.

4. (a) 16 minutes.

    (b) At 2:30.

    (c) No, it doesn't.

5. (a) A long time.

    (b) The Concord line.

    (c) Around the corner.

6. (a) You should fly there if you have the money.

    (b) It's about three thousand miles.

    (c) Yes, I can.

7. (a) It will take about an hour.

    (b) It's not very far from here.

    (c) You need to take the number 5 Express bus.

8. (a) Yes, that would be platform number 3.

    (b) No, I don't know when it stops.

    (c) Yes, it stops at midnight.

Exercise 2 **Directions:** You will hear six sentences. Read the three choices and circle the correct answer.

1. **(a)** The train will leave in twelve minutes.

    (b) The train will leave in two minutes.

    (c) The train will leave at two.

2. **(a)** The train is going to Yonkers.

    (b) The train is going to Grand Central Terminal.

    (c) The train will arrive in ten minutes.

3. **(a)** A one-way trip costs $2.90.

    (b) A one-way trip costs $1.45.

    (c) A round trip costs $2.19.

4. **(a)** The train will arrive in six minutes.

    (b) The train will arrive late.

    (c) The train will arrive at 12:10.

5. **(a)** The bus ride takes fifteen minutes.

    (b) There are four buses an hour.

    (c) The bus will come in fifteen minutes.

6. **(a)** The Fremont train takes half an hour.

    (b) You can get the Fremont train at platform number 4.

    (c) The Fremont train will be half an hour late.

Exercise 3 **Directions:** Listen to the conversation. Each time you hear the bell, read the statement and circle *True* or *False*.

1. The woman wants to help the man.   True   False

2. The woman wants to help the man.   True   False

3. The woman wants to help the man.   True   False

Exercise 4

Directions: You will hear three conversations. At the beginning of each conversation, you will hear a question. Listen to the conversation. Then, circle the best answer.

1. (a) Fremont.

   (b) Oakland West.

   (c) Oakland Coliseum.

2. (a) At 8:15.

   (b) In fifteen minutes.

   (c) At 8:10.

3. (a) Nothing.

   (b) $120.

   (c) $240.

Part VI   Using It: Planning a Vacation

Exercise

Directions: For this exercise, you will need to get some information outside of class. Decide with your teacher how many days you will have to gather your information.

As a class, choose a vacation city at least 1,000 miles away that you would all like to visit. Divide into groups. Each group will need to decide how and where to get its information and how best to share it with the class. Each group is responsible for one piece of the vacation puzzle and will share its information with the rest of the class. Be prepared to make charts and bring in any other materials that will help you with your presentations.

Group A: Airlines Contact at least four airlines. (All major airlines have toll-free telephone numbers.) Find out which airlines travel to your vacation city. For each airline, answer the following questions:

1. How much is a round-trip, coach fare (leaving on a Monday and returning the following Monday)?

2. How many flights are there to your vacation city on Monday mornings?

3. Are there any special discount rates?

4. How long will it take to reach your vacation city?

After comparing information, decide as a group which airline is best.

Group B: Train and Long-distance Bus Contact Amtrak and Greyhound Bus Company. Use the toll-free telephone number for each company to find information about travel to your vacation city. Answer the following questions:

1. How much is a round-trip ticket to your vacation city?
2. Are there any special discount rates?
3. Are there any express trains or buses to your city?
4. How long will it take to reach your vacation city?
5. What major cities will your trip take you through?
6. Are there toilets on board? Can you smoke, eat, or drink on board?

After comparing information, decide as a group which way to travel is best.

Group C: Places of Interest To get information about places of interest you can visit a travel agency, look at travel books, or interview people who are familiar with your vacation city. Choose at least four places of interest in your vacation city (museums, theme parks, national monuments, and so on). For each place, answer the following questions:

1. What kind of place is it?
2. What can people do there?
3. How much does it cost?
4. What hours is it open?
5. Where is it located?
6. Can you get there by public transportation?

Decide as a group which place sounds the most interesting.

Group D: Rental Cars Contact at least four different national rental car agencies about renting a car in your vacation city. (All national rental car agencies have toll-free telephone numbers.) For each agency, answer the following questions:

1. What is the price of a compact car in your vacation city for one week (Monday to Monday).
2. What is the price of a luxury sedan for one week (Monday to Monday).
3. Are there any special discounts available?
4. Is mileage free?
5. How much is the cheapest insurance for one week?

Decide as a group which agency and which kind of car is the best.

Group E: Hotel Accommodations Contact at least four national hotel chains to get the answers to the following questions. (All hotel chains have toll-free telephone numbers.) For each hotel, answer the following questions:

1. How much does a room for two people cost for one week (Monday to Monday)?
2. Can children stay for free?
3. How close is the hotel to the downtown area?
4. Does the hotel have a restaurant?
5. Does the hotel have free parking?
6. Are there any special rates available?

Decide as a group which hotel is the best.

CHAPTER THREE

Housing: "Good Neighbors"

Part I   Pre-listening: Housing Survey

Exercise 1   **Directions:** Check off all of the items which are true for your apartment, condominium, house, or dormitory.

A. Does your apartment, condominium, house, or dormitory have:	Yes	No
1. Good parking?		
2. Good views?		
3. Quiet neighbors?		
4. Enough privacy?		
5. Good plumbing and electricity?		
6. Enough fresh air and light?		
7. Central heating?		
8. Air conditioning?		
9. A reasonable rent?/monthly mortgage?		
10. Rent control?/fixed mortgage, and so on?		
11. Utilities included?		
12. A helpful landlord?/condo association?/dormitory advisor, and so on?		

B. Is your apartment, condominium, house, or dormitory:	Yes	No
1. Big enough for you?		
2. Safe?		
3. Near good transportation?		
4. Near schools and stores?		
5. Pest free? (no cockroaches, mice, or rats.)		

Exercise 2   **Directions:** Divide into pairs or small groups and compare and discuss your answers. Decide who has the best housing situation in the group and who has the worst housing situation. Give reasons for your choices.

Part II   Main Dialogue

Exercise 1   **Directions:** Listen to the dialogue and try to get a general idea of what is happening. Remember, you don't need to understand everything. Just try to think about the following questions:

- Where do you think the dialogue is taking place?
- Do the people in the dialogue know each other well?
- Think of several words to describe the two speakers.
- The dialogue is called "Good Neighbors." Is this dialogue *really* about "good neighbors"?

Exercise 2   **Directions:** Now, listen to the dialogue again to answer these questions:

rewind

1. Why doesn't David think the landlord will help him?
2. Which neighbor does he like?
3. What housing problem does Ruth have?
4. What is good about David's apartment?
5. Why don't the other neighbors help David?
6. Why doesn't David want to move?

Exercise 3   **Directions:** Listen to the dialogue one more time. Then, fill in the picture with the names of David's neighbors and the problems David is having with them. David doesn't talk about one of his neighbors. Put an *X* in that neighbor's apartment. Use letters and numbers from the following categories.

rewind

NAMES	PROBLEMS
A. Mrs. Gothe	**1.** Not taking out the garbage
B. Michael and Erica	**2.** Playing loud music
C. Rob and Steve	**3.** Fighting
D. Art	**4.** Talking loudly very early in the morning
	5. Noisy garbage collectors
	6. Having loud parties

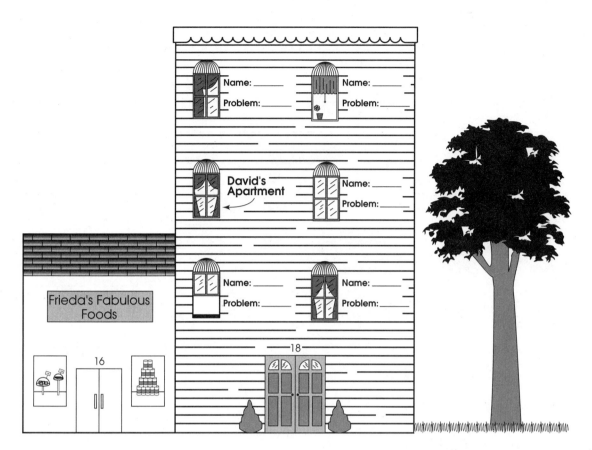

David's Apartment Building

Exercise 4

Directions: Listen to these sentences from the dialogue and circle the answer that has the same meaning.

1. **(a)** Michael and Erica were fighting.

   (b) Michael and Erica were out.

2. **(a)** He can charge more money.

   (b) He can get rid of rent control.

3. **(a)** That's terrible!

   (b) Tell me why.

4. **(a)** Her loud voice wakes me up at the same time every Sunday morning.

   (b) Her alarm clock wakes me up at the same time every Sunday morning.

5. **(a)** David feels sorry for her.

   (b) David thinks she has very little money.

6. **(a)** He isn't a nice person.

   (b) He doesn't take care of his apartment.

Exercise 5   **Directions:** David has different problems with each of his neighbors. In pairs or small groups, discuss the problems and write down what you would do to solve (find answers for) them.

Mrs. Gothe: _____

_____

Michael and Erica: _____

_____

Rob and Steve: _____

_____

Art: _____

_____

Part III   Expansion

Section 1 _____
Household Furnishings

Exercise 1A   **Directions:** Look at the figure of a floor plan of a three-room apartment. There are many different ways people choose to decorate their homes. Decide which of the things on the list below you would have in your home. Put each thing where you think it should go in the picture (you may put an item in more than one room).

drapes	linoleum	cabinets	window shades	window blinds
balcony	tiles	wallpaper	hardwood floors	mirrors
fireplace	carpeting	skylights	picture window	closets
rugs	curtains	deck	full-length mirrors	dishwasher

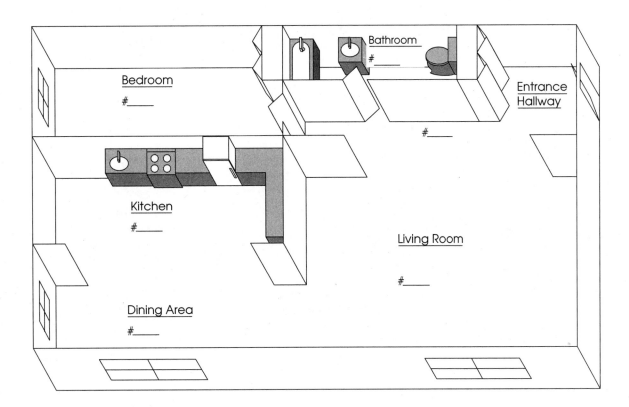

Floor Plan of a Three-Room Apartment

Now, compare your picture with a partner and discuss your choices.

Exercise 1B   **Directions:** Many people have problems with their homes. For example, they may have peeling paint or a stained carpet. In small groups, make a list of problems you have had with your homes. Then, discuss different ways to solve these problems.

PROBLEM   *SOLUTIONS*

_____   _____

                                                      _____

_____   _____

                                                      _____

_____   _____

                                                      _____

_____   _____

                                                      _____

Directions: Listen to the following conversations. Look at the picture of the three-room apartment and decide which room the people are in. Write the number of each conversation on the line in the correct room. Also, write down any words that help you.

Section 2 _____

Tenants' Rights

Exercise 2A

Directions: Read the following selection carefully. Underline any words you do not know, and try to guess the meanings. Discuss the meaning of their selection with your instructor.

When you rent an apartment or a house, you as a *tenant* have certain rights and responsibilities. Your *landlord* also has rights and responsibilities. A tenant and landlord often sign a *rental agreement* that lists some of these rights and responsibilities, but in many states, the tenant is also protected by certain laws. Most large cities have tenants' rights agencies to answer questions and help people. It is always important for the tenant to know what his or her rights are and what to do if there is a problem with the landlord.

For example, in most cities, the landlord is responsible for making sure the apartment or house is always in good condition. The landlord must repair any damage or problems that the tenant did not cause and make sure that:

1. There are no leaks when it rains and no broken doors or windows.
2. The plumbing works. There must be hot and cold water as well as a working sewer or septic tank connection.
3. The heater works and is safe.
4. The lights and wiring work and are safe.
5. Floors and stairways are in good repair.
6. There are enough garbage cans with covers.
7. The house or apartment is clean when the tenant moves in. The space must be free of rats, mice, roaches, or other pests, and there can't be any garbage in the house or apartment.

If your apartment or house has any of the above problems, the law says that you should do the following things:

1. Tell your landlord about the problem. Make sure that he or she knows exactly what's wrong. You can either talk to your landlord or write a letter. Writing a letter will protect your rights better than just talking.

2. Wait thirty days for the repairs to be made. If your problem is an emergency (for example, you have no heat in the winter), you only have to wait a few days.

3. If the landlord does not fix the problem within thirty days, have the repairs done yourself. Make sure you keep the receipts for all costs, and then deduct (subtract) the total amount from your next rental payment.

Sometimes tenants have problems when the landlord enters their apartment without telling them. In many cities, there are laws that protect a tenant's right of *privacy*. Your landlord cannot come into your apartment anytime he or she wants to. Your landlord must tell you at least twenty-four hours in advance that he or she is coming except in the following cases:

1. In an emergency.
2. When you have stopped paying rent and moved.
3. If a judge issues a court order.

If your landlord repeatedly comes into your apartment without telling you in advance, you may do the following things:

1. Write a letter to your landlord telling him or her not to enter your house or apartment without first giving you twenty-four hours notice. You can also ask that the landlord only visit you during normal business hours, Monday through Friday from 9:00 A.M. to 5:00 P.M.

2. Keep a list of the times that the landlord comes without advance warning. Talk to your neighbors and have them help watch your house or apartment.

3. Change the locks. The law does not say your landlord has to have a key to your apartment. But, if you do change your locks, you have to pay for it yourself, and you have to let the landlord in if he or she gives you twenty-four hours advance warning.

4. Call a tenants' rights agency in your city and ask them for legal help.

Because many tenants do not want to cause a fight with their land-lords, they don't complain when their landlords break the rules. Others may feel that the law cannot help them with their problems. But there are many laws that protect your rights, and it's important to know what they are. Find out about tenants' rights agencies in your area if you need help.

Exercise 2B

Directions: Listen to the following statements based on the reading passage. If the statement is true, circle *True* and if the statement is false, circle *False*.

1.	True	False	6.	True	False
2.	True	False	7.	True	False
3.	True	False	8.	True	False
4.	True	False	9.	True	False
5.	True	False	10.	True	False

Part IV Focus: Affirmative and Negative Yes/No Questions and Tag Questions

Your knowledge of structure and intonation is very important and can help you improve your listening skills. In this section, you will review *yes/no questions* and *tag questions*, both affirmative and negative. You already know about these different types of questions, but you still might get confused when you hear a negative yes/no question or a tag question. In the following exercise, you will focus on how understanding the differences between these kinds of questions will help you to improve your listening skills.

Look at the four questions in the box. Notice that the answers to *all* four questions are the same.

Type of question	Question	Possible situation	Response
Affirmative yes/no	Are you ESL students?	I have never met you before. I really do not know the answer.	Yes, we are.
Negative yes/no	Aren't you ESL students?	I think I remember you from another ESL class, but I'm not 100% sure.	Yes, we are.
Negative tag	You are ESL students, aren't you?	I think I remember you from another ESL class, but I'm not 100% sure.	Yes, we are.
Affirmative tag	You aren't ESL students, are you?	I think you look like Americans.	Yes, we are.

In all four questions, the speaker is asking for the same information: "Tell me 'yes' or 'no' if you are ESL students." The questions are the same. Only the situations are different.

The situation for the *affirmative yes/no question* is different from the other two types of questions. In the affirmative yes/no question, the speaker really does not know the answer and needs help.

The situations for the negative yes/no question, the affirmative tag question, and the negative tag question are really the same. In each situation, the speaker thinks that he or she knows the answer but wants to be sure that he or she is correct. When you hear negative yes/no questions or tag questions, do not let the negative auxiliaries confuse you.

Exercise 1

Directions: Listen to the following sentences. Decide whether they are affirmative yes/no questions, negative yes/no questions, affirmative tag questions, or negative tag questions. Check the correct box.

Example

Affirmative Yes/No	Negative Yes/No	Negative Tag	Affirmative Tag
		✓	

	Affirmative Yes/No	Negative Yes/No	Negative Tag	Affirmative Tag
1.				
2.				
3.				
4.				
5.				
6.				
7.				
8.				
9.				
10.				

Exercise 2

Directions: Listen to the same sentences. Then, choose the sentence that has the same meaning as the sentence you hear. Circle the correct letter.

Example (a) I think the rent is due on the first day of the month.

(b) I want to know if the rent is due on the first day of the month.

1. **(a)** I think a landlord can't throw you out without thirty days notice.

   (b) I want to know if a landlord can throw you out without thirty days notice.

2. **(a)** I think that you own your own home.

   (b) I want to know if you own your own home.

3. **(a)** I think you complained to the housing authority.

   (b) I want to know if you complained to the housing authority.

4. **(a)** I think your apartment had a view.

   (b) I want to know if your apartment had a view.

5. **(a)** I think utilities are included.

   (b) I want to know if utilities are included.

6. **(a)** I think the landlord can't evict you.

   (b) I think the landlord can evict you.

7. **(a)** I think you are going to stop paying your rent.

   (b) I want to know if you are going to stop paying your rent.

(Continued)

8. **(a)** I think you have a two-bedroom condominium.

(b) I think you don't have a two-bedroom condominium.

9. **(a)** I think Pete's apartment is under rent control.

(b) I think Pete's apartment isn't under rent control.

10. **(a)** I think Barbara refinished her hardwood floors.

(b) I want to know if Barbara refinished her hardwood floors.

Exercise 3A

Directions: Cindy Jameson is looking for an apartment. Yesterday, she spoke to a real estate agent about her situation. Listen to what she told the agent. Then, circle the correct answers on the chart.

Moved here from	Chicago / New York / Miami
Work location	Uptown / Midtown / Downtown
Wants apartment near	School / stores / buses
Car	Yes / No
Size of apartment wanted	Studio / one-bedroom / two-bedroom
Marital status	Single / married / divorced
Price of apartment wanted	$500–700/$800–1000/$1100–1300
Big kitchen wanted	Yes / No
Bathtub wanted	Yes / No
Furnished apartment wanted	Yes / No

Exercise 3B

Directions: The real estate agent has called Cindy back today to make sure that he remembers all of the information that Cindy gave him yesterday. Listen to the questions that he is asking Cindy and then circle the answer that Cindy should give.

Example (Yes, I do.)   No, I don't.

1. Yes, I do.   No, I don't.

2. Yes, I did.   No, I didn't.

3. Yes, I have.   No, I haven't.

4. Yes, I can.   No, I can't.

5. Yes, I do.   No, I don't.

6. Yes, I did.   No, I didn't.

7. Yes, I do.   No, I don't.

8. Yes, I will.   No, I won't.

9. Yes, I did.   No, I didn't.

10. Yes, I do.   No, I don't.

Part V   Listening Practice

Exercise 1

Directions: You will hear six sentences. Read the three possible responses and circle the correct answer.

1. **(a)** No, I'll do it next week.

   (b) Yes, I haven't moved yet.

   (c) No, I did it last week.

2. **(a)** Yes, I like my apartment very much.

   (b) It's a cute little one-bedroom with a porch.

   (c) Yes, my apartment has a lot of light.

3. **(a)** I don't want to deduct the repair costs from my rent.

   (b) I told him last week that my stove doesn't work.

   (c) I don't know, but he'd better do it within thirty days.

4. **(a)** The Millers are having another party.

   (b) The Millers are terrible neighbors.

   (c) The Millers come from Los Angeles.

5. **(a)** In the kitchen.

   (b) The sink is stopped up.

   (c) Yes, there's a terrible problem.

6. **(a)** Yes, I do.

   (b) Oh, very much.

   (c) No, but we're moving in June.

Exercise 2

Directions: You will hear seven sentences. Read the three choices and circle the correct answer.

1. (a) I will pay less rent next month.

   (b) I will pay more rent next month.

   (c) I won't pay any rent next month.

2. (a) I think it has rent control.

   (b) I think it doesn't have rent control.

   (c) I'm sure it doesn't have rent control.

3. (a) Mr. Thompson has had bad luck.

   (b) Mr. Thompson doesn't have much money.

   (c) Mr. Thompson cannot pay for heat.

4. (a) The studio has a garage.

   (b) The one-bedroom apartment has a view.

   (c) The studio has a view.

5. (a) Edward thinks Jeffrey is a mean person.

   (b) Edward thinks Jeffrey doesn't like to take care of his apartment.

   (c) Edward thinks Jeffrey is too noisy.

6. (a) You should call the tenants' union right now.

   (b) Your landlord should call the tenants' union right now.

   (c) You should call your landlord right now.

7. (a) Sam probably needs a garage.

   (b) Sam is probably single.

   (c) Sam is probably looking for a new job.

Exercise 3 **Directions:** Listen to the conversation. Each time you hear the bell, circle the sentence that you think is correct.

1. (a) Alice is happy where she lives.

   (b) Alice is not happy where she lives.

2. (a) Alice is happy where she lives.

   (b) Alice is not happy where she lives.

3. (a) Alice should buy a condo.

   (b) Alice should not buy a condo.

4. (a) Alice should not buy a condo.

   (b) Alice should buy a condo.

5. (a) Alice should rent an apartment.

   (b) Alice should not rent an apartment.

6. (a) Alice should rent an apartment.

   (b) Alice should buy a condo.

   (c) Alice should buy another house.

Exercise 4 **Directions:** You will hear three conversations. At the beginning of each conversation, you will hear a question. Listen to the conversation. Then, circle the best answer.

1. (a) A real estate agency

   (b) A tenants' rights agency

   (c) A rent control agency

2. (a) Four

   (b) Five

   (c) Six

3. (a) Adele

   (b) Rob

   (c) Both of them

Part VI   Using It: Solving Problems with Neighbors

Exercise 1   **Directions:** With a partner, read the following housing problems. For each problem, find a solution that would make both people in the situation happy.

1. Your neighbor who is also your best friend has a hearing problem and is very sensitive about the problem. Each night he or she plays the television very loudly and doesn't know that it bothers you. You are afraid to hurt your neighbor's feelings, but you finally decide that you need to talk to him or her.

2. Your bank lost your paycheck. The rent is three days late, but the bank cannot help you for another week. Your landlord knows that you are a responsible and very good tenant, but needs your money to pay the mortgage.

3. Your next-door neighbor is a musician and makes money by giving music lessons in his or her apartment. He or she teaches during the day and several evenings each week. The noise is very annoying, but your neighbor does not have enough money to rent a classroom. You like your neighbor very much, but cannot stand the noise anymore.

4. Your neighbor works until midnight and doesn't get home until about 1:00 am. Parking in your neighborhood is very difficult and sometimes when your neighbor cannot find a parking space, he or she parks in front of your garage. You go to work early each day and cannot get your car out of the garage when your neighbor is parked there. You like your neighbor and understand how bad the parking problem is, but you have already been late to work three times.

5. You have lived in your apartment for ten years and it needs to be repainted. You ask your landlord to do it. Your landlord agrees that the apartment needs new paint, but also feels that if your apartment is painted, the other tenants will also want new paint jobs and he or she cannot afford to do that.

Exercise 2   **Directions:** Choose one of the five housing problems in Exercise 1, a problem from the Main Dialogue, or a problem of your own. With your partner, role-play the problem. Make sure that you speak to each other for at least two minutes. After you have practiced your role play, present it to the class.

CHAPTER FOUR

Medical Needs and Services: "A Healthy Excuse"

Part I   Pre-listening: Medicine Cabinet

Exercise 1   **Directions:** In pairs or small groups, look at the items in the picture of the medicine cabinet and decide in which category of the chart on page 44 each item belongs. The first one is done for you. When you are finished, put a check next to each item that must have dosage information.

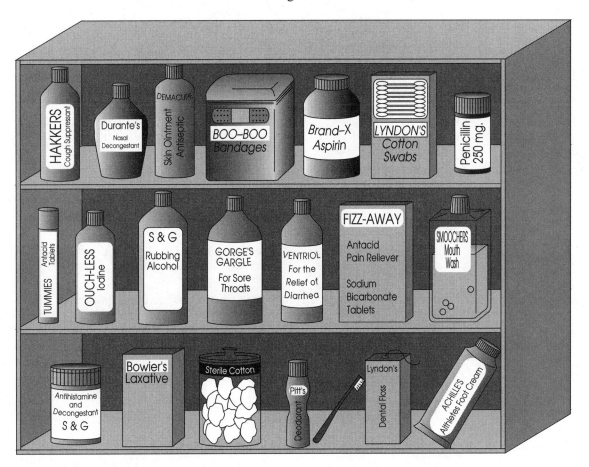

Medicine cabinet

Categories

Stomach	Personal hygiene	Cold/flu/allergy	First aid	Antibiotics
	deodorant			

Part II   Main Dialogue

Exercise 1

Directions: Listen to the dialogue and try to get a general idea of what is happening. Remember, you don't need to understand everything. Just try to think about the following questions:

- Where do you think this dialogue is taking place?

  Describe what you think the place looks like. Give as many details as you can.

- What is the relationship between the people in the dialogue?

- When do you think this dialogue takes place (time of day, time of year, and so on)?

Exercise 2

rewind

Directions: Now, listen to the dialogue again to answer these questions:

1. What does Christine say is her problem?
2. What did Christine do last night?
3. Christine's mother is worried that Christine did something bad last night. What was it?
4. Why does Christine's mother want to call the doctor?
5. Who calls Christine? Why?
6. What is Christine's *real* problem?

Directions: Look at the following chart of symptoms. Discuss any new vocabulary with your teacher.

Symptoms of Illness

Symptom		Symptom	
Fever/temperature		Chills/shivering	
Vomiting		Rash	
Stomach ache		Dizziness	
Earache		Back ache	
Headache		Cramps	
Gas pains		Diarrhea	
Heartburn		Nausea	
Constipation		Sore throat	
Nasal congestion		Runny nose	

rewind

Directions: Listen to the dialogue one more time. While you are listening, put a check next to each symptom that you hear mentioned in the dialogue.

Exercise 4   **Directions:**   Listen to these sentences from the dialogue and circle the answer that has the same meaning.

1. (a) I feel a little sick.

    (b) I am tired of the cold weather.

2. (a) I'm sure you know that drunk driving causes car accidents.

    (b) I'm sure you know that alcohol can make young people sick.

3. (a) Kids do bad things so their friends will like them.

    (b) Kids like to go out and be in big crowds.

4. (a) Please let me rest.

    (b) Please stop bothering me.

5. (a) Many people have been getting the same sickness.

    (b) You must feel very dizzy.

6. (a) Your throat has redness.

    (b) Your throat doesn't have redness.

7. (a) I don't know how to take care of you.

    (b) I don't think that you are sick.

Exercise 1A   **Directions:** The class will be divided into pairs of students. Each member of the pair will look at his or her own chart with information about symptoms, illnesses, and possible treatments. Student A will look only at Chart A. Student B will look only at Chart B. Each student will have missing information that his or her partner can supply. For example, if you are missing the name of the first illness on the chart, ask your partner for the name of the illness. Then, fill in the information on your chart. Do *not* look at your partner's chart. If you don't know how to spell a word ask your partner to spell it for you. If you have trouble with the vocabulary, ask your teacher for help.

Chart A

	Possible symptoms	Name of illness	Possible treatments
1.		Flu	Aspirin / nasal spray / cough suppressant / bed rest
2.	Sneezing / rash / trouble breathing / itchy, swelling eyes		Antihistamines / injections
3.	Red spots all over body / itching	Measles	
4.	Lumps / rectal bleeding /weight loss / blue or black skin growths / swelling under armpits or in throat		Radiation treatment (X-ray)/ chemotherapy / surgical removal of tumors
5.	Very high fever / difficulty breathing / chills / coughing	Pneumonia	
6.		Poison oak / ivy	Creams / lotions / antihistamines / injections
7.		Ulcers	Oral medication to coat stomach sores / surgery
8.	Shortness of breath / chest pains / nausea		Surgery / oral medications/ easier living
9.	Night sweats / sudden weight loss / loss of appetite	AIDS	
10.	Difficulty breathing / no fever	Asthma	
11.	Unusual thirst / frequent urination		Special no-sugar diet / insulin injections
12.	Difficulty bending joints (arms, legs, fingers, and so on)	Arthritis	

Chart B

Possible symptoms	Name of illness	Possible treatments
1. Fever / chills / runny nose / sore throat	Flu	
2.	Allergy	Antihistamines / injections
3. Red spots all over body / itching		Bed rest / keep patient away from other people, especially pregnant women
4. Lumps / rectal bleeding / weight loss / blue or black skin growths / swelling under armpits or in throat	Cancer	
5.	Pneumonia	Antibiotics / bed rest
6. Itching / runny blisters / no fever		Creams / lotions / antihistamines / injections
7. Indigestion / sharp, stabbing pain in stomach	Ulcers	
8.	Heart trouble	Surgery / oral medications / easier living
9. Night sweats / Sudden weight loss / loss of appetite		No long-term treatment
10.	Asthma	Move to climate with clean, dry air / special inhalers to help with breathing
11.	Diabetes	Special no-sugar diet / insulin injections
12. Difficulty bending joints (arms, legs, fingers, and so on)		Injections / pain killers

Exercise 1B   **Directions:** Look at the chart and listen to the following dialogues. For each

dialogue, first circle the symptoms that the people are talking about. Second, circle the actions that the people take to feel better. Finally, write down the name of the illness or condition that you think the people in the dialogue have. Do not worry about spelling.

Symptoms	Actions	Condition/illness
Dialogue 1. Diarrhea / vomiting / chills / upset stomach / stuffy nose	Antibiotic / bed rest / visit doctor / nasal spray / drink fluids	
Dialogue 2. Rash / fever / itching / broken leg	Aspirin / skin cream / no touching / bed rest	
Dialogue 3. Headache / indigestion / constipation / diarrhea	Visit doctor / antacid / drink fluids / antibiotics	

Section 2
AIDS

Exercise 2A   **Directions:** Read the following passage and discuss the meaning with your instructor.

We have talked about many different kinds of illnesses so far in this chapter. Some of these illnesses are temporary and not very serious, while others are chronic and very dangerous. One disease that has killed many people is called AIDS. It is very important for you to know about this illness.

WHAT IS AIDS?

AIDS stands for <u>A</u>cquired (not born with) <u>I</u>mmune (your body's ability to fight disease) <u>D</u>eficiency (not working properly) <u>S</u>yndrome (a group of signs and symptoms). A virus called *HIV* causes AIDS. The AIDS virus can affect people in different ways. People carrying HIV can give the virus to others, even if they don't have any symptoms. It can take several years for any signs of the illness to appear. People with AIDS often get sick with many illnesses that their bodies are not able to fight. Some of the diseases are fatal, and there is no cure for AIDS right now.

HOW DO PEOPLE GET AIDS?

AIDS is very difficult to get. It is *not* contagious like a cold or the flu. It is only spread through *blood* and *sex*. People who are *at risk* for AIDS:

1. Have unsafe sex (sex without a condom) with someone who is infected with the AIDS virus.
2. Share intravenous (I.V.) needles with someone who is infected with the AIDS virus.
3. Receive blood transfusions or blood products from someone infected with the AIDS virus. (Since 1985, tests have been used to make sure that the blood supply is safe.)
4. Are born to a woman infected with the AIDS virus.

YOU *CANNOT* GET AIDS BY:

1. Going to a public event or riding public transportation.
2. Eating in restaurants.
3. Swimming in public pools.
4. Being bitten by an insect.
5. Sharing clothing, dishes, food, or toilet seats with someone who has AIDS.
6. Coughing or sneezing; hugging or playing with someone who has AIDS.
7. Donating blood to a blood bank.

WHAT ARE THE SYMPTOMS OF AIDS?

At first, the symptoms of AIDS can look like common illnesses such as a cold or the flu. Some of the symptoms are:

1. Chronic (lasting a long time) diarrhea.
2. Fever, chills, or night sweats lasting longer than several weeks.
3. Extreme weight loss (losing more than ten pounds) without a reason.
4. Swollen glands in the neck or under the arms lasting more than two weeks.
5. White spots or sores in the mouth.
6. Dry cough or shortness of breath.
7. Memory loss or confusion.

Remember, these symptoms are common in other illnesses as well. With AIDS, however, these symptoms can last longer or be much more serious. If you have these symptoms, you should see a doctor.

HOW CAN I FIND OUT IF I HAVE THE AIDS VIRUS?

To find out if you have the AIDS virus there is a special blood test you can take called the HIV Antibody Test. Most communities have health centers listed in your telephone book, where you can take the test for free. If the test result is *positive*, it means that you have the AIDS virus. If the test result is *negative*, it means that you do not have the AIDS virus.

CAN AIDS BE TREATED?

There is no cure for AIDS at this time. So, most people with AIDS die. However, many of the illnesses people get when they have AIDS can be treated. Some treatments are helping people live longer and more comfortably.

HOW CAN I PROTECT MYSELF FROM AIDS?

1. Always have safe sex (always use a condom).
2. If you use drugs, never share needles.

The best way to protect yourself from getting AIDS is to make sure that you know the facts about how this disease is, and is *not*, spread. If you share this information with your family and friends, fewer people will be at risk for this disease.

Exercise 2B

Directions: Listen to the following conversations and decide whether or not the people speaking or being spoken about are at risk for getting AIDS. Circle your answer.

1. At risk

   Not at risk

2. At risk

   Not at risk

3. At risk

   Not at risk

Part IV   Focus: Stress and Intonation

English makes use of *stress* and *intonation* to add meaning to sentences. Stress usually means that a word has a rising change in pitch and an increase in loudness and length. Stress is used for many reasons.

Section 1
Word Stress

Normal sentence stress indicates the most important word or words in the sentence.

Examples   Bob is a **doctor.**

Heart disease is **the leading cause** of death in the United States.

Dr. Adams is visiting a patient at **City Hospital.**

When we change the stressed word or words in a sentence, the meaning of the sentence changes. Stress can show contrast, emotion, or clarification.

C O N T R A S T

When a speaker wants to tell a listener that what the speaker has just said is incorrect, he or she stresses the word or words in the sentence that give the correct information.

Examples
1. **Bob** is a doctor. (not *Tom*)

2. **Heart disease** is the leading cause of death in the United States. (not *cancer*)

3. Dr. Adams is **visiting** the patient in Room 411. (not *treating* the patient.)

E M O T I O N

A speaker can also use stress to show emotions (feelings) such as shock (strong surprise), anger, or sarcasm.

Examples
1. Phil is in **the hospital?** (shock)

2. The nurse gave him **the wrong medicine!** (anger)

3. This medicine tastes **just like candy.** (sarcasm)

C L A R I F I C A T I O N

In addition, when a speaker is unsure of having heard the correct information, he or she uses stress to ask for clarification.

Examples
1. Your temperature is ninety-**nine**-point-six? (not ninety-*eight*-point-six?)

2. Do you spell that p-e-n-i-<u>c</u>-i-l-l-i-n? (not with an <u>s</u>?)

3. Louise is in **Kings** County Hospital? (Not *Queens* County Hospital)

Exercise 1A   **Directions:** Listen to the following sentences, and underline the word with the greatest stress in each sentence.

1. Ted went to the doctor because he had a throat infection?
2. Tony waited until he had a fever of 102 before he went to the doctor!
3. Cancer is the number two killer of people in the United States.
4. The medicine is under the cabinet?
5. Liz went to a skin specialist.
6. The antibiotic costs twenty-nine ninety five?
7. Cindy found out that she has diabetes!
8. Dr. Dryer is such a wonderful doctor!
9. That doctor gives pills for everything!
10. They will give you an X-ray to check for that disease.

Exercise 1B   **Directions:** Listen to these sentences again and decide whether the stressed words indicate contrast, emotion, or clarification. Check the correct box.

	Contrast	Emotion	Clarification
1.			
2.			
3.			
4.			
5.			
6.			
7.			
8.			
9.			
10.			

Section 2
Number Stress

Many non-native English speakers have trouble hearing the difference between numbers in the teens (*thirteen, fourteen, fifteen,* and so on) and numbers in increments of ten (*thirty, forty, fifty,* and so on). English uses stress to clarify the difference between these numbers.

For numbers in the teens, the stress is always on the second syllable: *teen*.

Example   He was in the hospital for four***teen*** days.

For numbers in increments of ten, the stress is always on the first syllable.

Example   He was in the hospital for *for*ty days.

As you can see, the stress and meanings are both very different.

Exercise 2

Directions: Listen to the following sentences. Circle the number you hear.

1.	(a) 15	(b) 50	**6.**	(a) 14	(b) 40
2.	(a) 15	(b) 50	**7.**	(a) 16	(b) 60
3.	(a) 1335	(b) 3035	**8.**	(a) 17	(b) 70
4.	(a) 13	(b) 30	**9.**	(a) 19	(b) 90
5.	(a) 14	(b) 40	**10.**	(a) 18	(b) 80

Exercise 3

Directions: Listen to the following sentences and choose the sentence that would best follow each one in a normal dialogue. Circle the correct answer.

Examples   1.   **(a)**   Are you really sure? I thought I could phone it in.

   (b)   Are you really sure? I thought I had to go to Metro Pharmacy.

2.   **(a)**   Are you really sure? I thought I could phone it in.

   (b)   Are you really sure? I thought I had to go to Metro Pharmacy.

1.   (a) Nineteen dollars is a good price.

   (b) Ninety dollars is much too much money!

2.   (a) That's strange. John said she was going to nursing school.

   (b) I thought your son was going to be the doctor.

3.   (a) That's strange. John said she was going to nursing school.

   (b) I thought your son was going to be the doctor.

4.   (a) Yes, it's on the 5th.

   (b) Yes, it's in March.

5.   (a) I agree. It's the best.

   (b) I know. It's really bad.

6.   (a) Oh, I'm sorry. I thought he needed a dentist.

   (b) Oh, I thought *you* were the patient.

7.   (a) Oh, I'm sorry. I thought he needed a dentist.

   (b) Oh, I thought *you* were the patient.

8.   (a) That's too much money.

   (b) That's really cheap.

(Continued)

9. (a) I know. I can't believe that he is dead!

    (b) Oh, so his wife is the sick one.

10. (a) I know. I can't believe that he is dead!

    (b) Oh, so his wife is the sick one.

Part V   Listening Practice

Exercise 1

Directions: You will hear seven questions. Read the three possible responses and circle the correct answer.

1. (a) A fever of 102 degrees.

    (b) A little under the weather.

    (c) Yes, I am.

2. (a) Yes, a lot.

    (b) Sneezing, runny nose, and chills.

    (c) I bought Hakker's cough suppressant.

3. (a) Yes, and we got some medicine right away.

    (b) No, she's never had that disease.

    (c) No, she'll get one when she starts school.

4. (a) He told me to get some aspirin.

    (b) She suggested that I use some rubbing alcohol.

    (c) He wants me to take penicillin.

5. (a) Call 911.

    (b) Take a laxative.

    (c) Try some antacid tablets.

6. (a) Some bandages and sterile cotton.

    (b) Some mouth wash and dental floss.

    (c) Some deodorant and athlete's foot cream.

7. (a) Yes, I've heard there is.

    (b) I don't know. We should ask a doctor.

    (c) I think it's easy to catch that disease.

Directions: You will hear seven sentences. Read the three choices and circle the correct answer.

1. **(a)** It's my daughter, not my son.

   (b) She has the measles, not another illness.

   (c) She's at home, not in the hospital.

2. **(a)** She has AIDS.

   (b) She has diabetes.

   (c) She has cancer.

3. **(a)** I owe you fifty cents.

   (b) I owe you eighty-five cents.

   (c) I owe you fifteen cents.

4. **(a)** It might be a stomach virus.

   (b) It might be arthritis.

   (c) It might be ulcers.

5. **(a)** She will probably have the disease for a long time.

   (b) She will probably die from this disease.

   (c) She will probably get better soon.

6. **(a)** The doctors don't know what Mr. Mason's symptoms are.

   (b) The doctors don't think that Mr. Mason is sick.

   (c) The doctors don't know how to help Mr. Mason.

7. **(a)** They probably both have colds.

   (b) Bob probably has a cold.

   (c) Jerry probably has a cold.

Exercise 3

Directions: Listen to the conversation. Each time you hear the bell, read the statement and circle *True* or *False*.

1. The woman probably has a serious medical problem.   True   False

2. The woman probably has a serious medical problem.   True   False

3. The woman's sister has a serious medical problem.   True   False

4. The woman's sister has a serious medical problem.   True   False

5. The baby has a serious medical problem.   True   False

Exercise 4 **Directions:** You will hear four conversations. At the beginning of each conversation, you will hear a question. Listen to the conversation. Then, circle the best answer.

1. (a) Cancer

   (b) Stomach flu

   (c) A cold

2. (a) Diarrhea

   (b) Chills

   (c) Fever

3. (a) She's probably sick.

   (b) She probably needs a checkup.

   (c) She probably needs a vaccination.

4. (a) He has allergy problems.

   (b) He needs a checkup.

   (c) He is sick.

Part VI   Using It: AIDS Prevention Awareness Campaign

AIDS is a very serious disease that more and more people are dying from. It is therefore very important that people get correct information to stop the spread of this disease. In this exercise, you will put together an advertising program to teach people how to protect themselves and their loved ones from HIV infection.

Exercise **Directions:** After your instructor has divided the class into groups, choose one of the following advertising methods to put together an advertisement that you believe would interest as many people as possible. Refer back to Part III, Section 2 of this chapter for specific information about AIDS and AIDS prevention that you might want to include in your ad. After your group has finished, present the ad to the class.

Group A: Radio announcement Create a one-minute radio announcement about AIDS prevention and awareness. Be careful in choosing your words! Remember that for radio, only spoken words and music can be used.

Group B: TV Announcement Create a one-minute TV announcement. Make sure that you include interesting action and visual aids. Remember that television uses pictures and sound together.

Group C: Poster Create a poster that really catches the eye. Make sure that the information is clear and easy to understand and that it leaves the reader thinking about the topic. Choose your words and pictures very carefully.

Try to be creative. Your goal is to get people to become aware and interested in this very important topic. You can be very serious in your ad or you might use humor. In either case, you want your announcement to get a lot of attention.

CHAPTER FIVE

Shopping: "Which One Is the Better Buy?"

Part I   Pre-listening: Consumer Awareness

Exercise 1   **Directions:** In pairs or small groups, look at the picture of a television advertisement and then answer the questions on page 58.

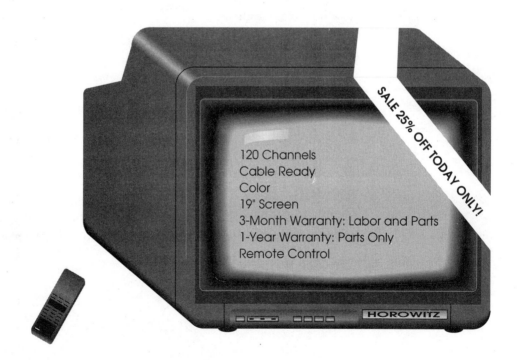

1. What brand of TV is this?

   List three other brands of TVs that you know.

   _____   _____   _____

2. How much is the discount if you buy this TV today?

3. Does this TV come with a wireless remote control?

4. What kinds of stores sell TVs?

5. Which of the following features does this TV have?

   a. remote control, black and white, 90-day guarantee

   b. color, 120 channels, 19"-screen

   c. cable ready, stereo, color

6. For how long will the company repair this TV for free? For how long will they replace broken parts for free?

7. What features does your TV at home have?

8. Do you have cable TV? Why or why not? What is different about cable TV?

Part II   Main Dialogue

Exercise 1

Directions: Listen to the dialogue and try to get a general idea of what is happening. Remember, you don't need to understand everything. Just try to think about the following questions:

- Where do you think this dialogue is taking place?
- Do you think the speakers know each other? Why or why not?
- Think of several words to describe the two speakers.

Exercise 2

rewind

Directions: Now, listen to the dialogue again to answer these questions:

1. How many televisions do the customer and salesperson talk about?

2. How many brands do they talk about?

3. Why are Sony TVs good?

4. What kind of TV does the salesperson recommend for good sound?

5. Which TV does the customer think is best for her?

6. How does the salesperson feel at the end of the conversation? Explain.

Exercise 3

Directions: Listen to the dialogue one more time. Then, fill in the chart with information about the TVs.

rewind

Brand	Size	Price	Cable ready	Stereo	Warranty
SONY					
Panasonic 1					
Zenith					
Panasonic 2					

Exercise 4

Directions: Listen to these sentences from the dialogue and circle the answer that has the same meaning.

1. **(a)** Does the Sony give me more for its price?

   (b) Is the Sony cheaper?

2. **(a)** The Panasonic is O.K.

   (b) The Panasonic is good, too.

3. **(a)** You should listen to a stereo TV.

   (b) You should buy a stereo TV.

4. **(a)** How many years will a cable-ready stereo TV last?

   (b) How much does a cable-ready stereo TV cost?

5. **(a)** Which TV gives me more for its price?

   (b) Which TV has a better picture?

6. **(a)** It's easier to make it work.

   (b) It's difficult to use.

Part III Expansion

Section 1
In the Supermarket

Exercise 1A **Directions:** In pairs or small groups, study and discuss the following floor plan of a supermarket. Then, answer the questions on page 61. If there are any words that you don't understand, ask your instructor for help.

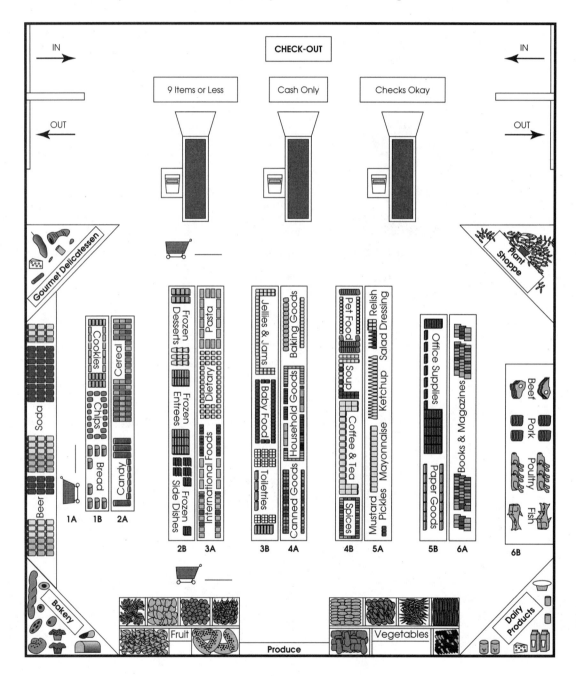

Floor Plan of a Supermarket

1. There are three places in the store where you can find beans. Where are they? There are three places where you can find fruit. Where are they?

2. In which sections would you find labels with expiration dates? In which sections would you find foods that are domestic or imported? In which sections would you find perishable foods?

3. Where can you find things to clean your bathroom? Where can you find things to clean your body?

4. The store is closing in two minutes and you have to buy food for dinner. You only have time to go down one aisle. Which aisle would you go to and what would you choose?

5. John is walking to the check-out stand. His basket is full of items he wishes to purchase. In the chart below, write the aisle number from which he found each item.

Item	Aisle number
A pound of chicken	
Two loaves of bread	
A bouquet of roses	
A notebook	
A tube of toothpaste	
A pound of flour	
A quart of milk	
A bag of Japanese crackers	
A can of cleanser	

6. Tell your group about shopping for food in your native country. Are the stores the same as they are in the United States? If not, how are they different? Which stores do you prefer?

Exercise 1B **Directions:** Listen to the following conversations. Then, put the number of the conversation next to the place on the picture of the store where the conversation took place.

Section 2
Store Rules

Exercise 2A **Directions:** With your instructor, read the store policy on page 62. Talk about what each rule means and decide why the store has the rule. Finally, decide in what kind of store you would find these rules.

Store Policy

```
┌─────────────────────────────────────────────────┐
│                  Store Policy                   │
│                 ─────────────                    │
│   1. Check all bags at the counter.             │
│                                                  │
│   2. No eating or drinking in store.            │
│                                                  │
│   3. No smoking.                                 │
│                                                  │
│   4. No cash refunds.                            │
│                                                  │
│   5. Returns with receipt only within seven days.│
│                                                  │
│   6. No more than three garments in the dressing │
│      room at one time.                           │
│                                                  │
│   7. Only VISA and Mastercard accepted.          │
│                                                  │
│   8. Checks accepted with valid ID  only.        │
│                                                  │
│   9. Shoplifters will be prosecuted.             │
└─────────────────────────────────────────────────┘
```

Store Policy

Exercise 2B

Directions: Listen to the following conversations. Then, choose the store policy that applies. Circle the correct answer.

1. **(a)** Check all bags at the counter.

    (b) No cash refunds.

    (c) Checks accepted with valid ID only.

    (d) Only VISA and Mastercard accepted.

2. **(a)** No cash refunds.

    (b) Checks accepted with valid ID only.

    (c) Only VISA and Mastercard accepted.

    (d) Shoplifters will be prosecuted.

3. **(a)** Check all bags at the counter.

    (b) No more than three garments in the dressing room at one time.

    (c) No eating or drinking in store.

    (d) Returns with receipt only within seven days.

Part IV   Focus: Contrast and Concession

You already know most of the conjunctions in English (*and, or, but, so, although, before, after,* and so on). Conjunctions show how the ideas in one sentence or clause are related to the ideas in another sentence or clause.

Your knowledge of conjunctions can help improve your listening skills.

When you hear a sentence or clause with a conjunction in it, you can guess the kind of information that is going to follow. Even if you don't know all of the words in the sentence or clause, you can often guess the meaning because of the information that the conjunction gives you.

Look at the following unfinished sentence from the dialogue:

"It is a good price, *but* _____ ."

The conjunction *but* joins two sentences. When you see the word *but*, you know that the second clause will show a contrast to the first clause in some way.

Which of the following clauses can follow the first half of the above sentence? Remember that they must show a contrast to the first clause.

It is a good price, but _____ .

a. remember that it isn't cable ready.

b. it is on sale.

c. it won't be on sale until next week.

d. remember it also has the best color.

Choice *a* is a good contrast. From the first clause, *It is a good price*, we expect something good. *Remember that it isn't cable ready* indicates something that is not good.

Choice *b* is not a good contrast. Like the first clause *it is on sale* describes something good.

Choice *c* is good for the same reason as choice *a*.

Choice *d*, like choice *b*, does not show a contrast.

But can also show concession (or an unexpected result).

A speaker uses **concession** to tell a listener that he or she is going to hear something unexpected.

Example   *"The Sony is an unbeatable price, but if cable-ready is important, you might consider the Panasonic."*

Here, the listener expects to hear that the Sony is the best buy. The speaker uses *but* to introduce the idea that the Panasonic might actually be another good choice. This is *concession*.

Other words that are similar to *but* are *even though* and *although*.

Example   *Even though* the store only sells second-hand clothes, the prices are quite high.

The listener probably thinks that used clothes are inexpensive. That is not true at this store. The speaker says that the prices are actually high.

Now practice using your knowledge of these conjunctions to help improve your listening skills.

Exercise 1

Directions: Listen to the following clauses and decide which clauses can be joined to them. Circle the correct answer.

Example   **(a)**   I bought something.

            (b)   I spent money.

            (c)   I didn't buy anything.

Only answer *c* makes sense. The other two do not show any contrast or concession. Answer *c* is in contrast to what the listener expects.

1.   (a) I bought a Panasonic.

     (b) I bought a new one.

     (c) they were on sale.

2.   (a) the store threw the milk away.

     (b) the store sold the milk.

     (c) the store ordered more milk.

3.   (a) I really had to exchange them.

     (b) I bought them anyway.

     (c) I tried them on.

4.   (a) it was beautiful.

     (b) it wasn't the right color.

     (c) it was a good deal.

5.   (a) she wanted to pay with a check.

     (b) she was finished shopping.

     (c) she was in the express line.

6.   (a) I still don't have time to shop.

     (b) it is very convenient.

     (c) I go whenever I want to.

7.   (a) he didn't have a lot of cash.

     (b) he had plenty of cash.

     (c) he will pay for it at the end of the month.

8.   (a) his old one broke down.

     (b) his old one needed a lot of repairs.

     (c) his old one was still good.

9.   (a) you should buy it.

     (b) I think it is too expensive.

     (c) it is the perfect color.

10.   (a) their shoes will be 40 percent off.

     (b) their shoes won't be on sale.

     (c) their shoes will be cheaper.

Exercise 2   **Directions:** Listen to the following sentences. Circle the correct answer.

Example   **(a)** I like the produce.

(**b**) I don't like the produce.

(c) I don't like Turner's.

We already know that answer *c* is incorrect because the first part of the statement says that the service is wonderful. The first clause tells us something good about the store, so the second clause introduced by *but* must show contrast or concession. Even if you didn't know the word *produce*, you would still be able to guess that answer *b* is correct because of the contrast or concession that *but* shows. Answer *b* is therefore the correct answer.

1. **(a)** The store had good prices.

    (b) The customer wasn't happy.

    (c) The customer bought something on sale.

2. **(a)** I think you should buy the imported cheese.

    (b) I think you should buy the domestic cheese.

    (c) I think you should buy both cheeses.

3. **(a)** Department stores are the best place to shop.

    (b) There are better places to shop than department stores.

    (c) It's good to look for department store sales.

4. **(a)** The Mitsubishi didn't have a good warranty.

    (b) The Toshiba had a good warranty.

    (c) The warranty wasn't important to me.

5. **(a)** Spinelli's prices are cheap.

    (b) I am unhappy with Spinelli's.

    (c) Spinelli's isn't popular.

6. **(a)** The customer probably bought the suit.

    (b) The suit wasn't good for the customer's needs.

    (c) The suit was good for the customer's needs.

7. **(a)** You should always shop at Cottonworth's.

    (b) You shouldn't shop at Cottonworth's.

    (c) You should shop at Cottonworth's only when they have sales.

8. **(a)** There is something bad about hamburgers.

    (b) There is nothing bad about hamburgers.

    (c) Maybe there is something bad about hamburgers.

Part V   Listening Practice

Directions: You will hear seven questions. Read the three possible responses and circle the correct answer.

1. (a) This brand has four more ounces.

    (b) We sell Kellogg's, Honey Bran, and Cheerios.

    (c) I'm sorry. We don't have any.

2. (a) We'll have one in three months.

    (b) It's good for three months.

    (c) We have sold that one for three months.

3. (a) It has 131 channels.

    (b) It will be ready soon.

    (c) Yes, it is.

4. (a) About $14,000.

    (b) 120 miles per hour.

    (c) One year or 12,000 miles.

5. (a) 19 inches.

    (b) 131 channels.

    (c) Cable-ready.

6. (a) No, it's too expensive.

    (b) I guess I'll use my VISA.

    (c) Yes, I've already paid.

7. (a) Yes, you can.

    (b) It looks beautiful!

    (c) In the dressing room.

Exercise 2 **Directions:** You will hear seven sentences. Read the three choices and circle the correct answer.

1. (a) I suggest you buy the Chevrolet.

   (b) I suggest you buy either a Chevrolet or a Honda.

   (c) You'd better buy the Honda.

2. (a) Each TV is 19 inches.

   (b) Each TV is stereo.

   (c) Each TV is cable ready.

3. (a) It costs $182.

   (b) It costs $329.

   (c) It costs $130.

4. (a) The Volkswagen costs less than the Ford.

   (b) The Ford will go faster than the Volkswagen.

   (c) The Ford costs less than the Volkswagen.

5. (a) The price was cheaper at the supermarket.

   (b) The supermarket had a sale.

   (c) The price was cheaper at the corner store.

6. (a) You should buy the blue sweater.

   (b) The blue sweater will keep you warm.

   (c) You ought to buy a different sweater.

7. (a) I will probably buy the beer.

   (b) I probably won't buy the beer.

   (c) I might buy the beer.

Directions: You will hear four conversations. At the beginning of each conversation, you will hear a question. Listen to the conversation. Then, circle the best answer.

1. **(a)** $650.

   (b) two days.

   (c) $500.

2. **(a)** A 24-inch color Sony.

   (b) A 13-inch cable ready Zenith.

   (c) A 12-inch color Panasonic.

3. **(a)** A 50-percent silk blouse, imported from Italy.

   (b) A 100-percent satin blouse, imported from China.

   (c) A 100-percent silk blouse, imported from China.

4. **(a)** The Pepsi.

   (b) The Coke.

   (c) They're the same.

Exercise 4

Directions: Listen to the speaker describe her day. Then, put the chores in the correct order. Cross out any chore that the speaker is *not* planning to do.

Go to the doctor	Go to the supermarket	Vacuum the floors
Go to the cleaners	Go to the library	Clean the bathroom
Put away the groceries	Cook dinner	Water the plants

Part VI   Using It: Comparison Shopping

In our modern society, consumers (shoppers) have many choices. Because there are so many choices, people are often confused about how to find the best deal. In this exercise, you will go out into your community and compare similar stores to see which store is the best one to shop at.

Exercise

Directions: Decide with your teacher how many days the class will have to gather information. After your teacher has divided the class into groups, follow the instructions below for your group only. After you have gathered the information, decide as a group which store is the best and then explain to the rest of the class how you reached your decision.

Group A: Find three department stores in your area. For each department store find the following information:

1. Name of store.
2. Location of store.
3. Store hours.
4. Return policy.
5. Does the store accept credit cards? If so, which ones?
6. Does the store have a restaurant? If so, what is the price of a hamburger and a small soda?
7. What is the price of a pair of men's 501 Levi blue jeans?
8. What is the price of a small bottle of Chanel No. 5 perfume?
9. Will this store mail packages for you?
10. Describe two things about this store that you think are special.

Group B: Find three stores that sell groceries in your area. For each store find the following information:

1. Name of store.
2. Location of store.
3. Store hours.
4. How many aisles are there in the store?
5. Does the store have a deli? If so, what kinds of food does the deli sell?
6. Will this store deliver groceries to a customer's home?
7. Besides cash, what other ways can customers pay for groceries in this store?
8. What is the price of a seven-ounce box of Kellogg's Corn Flakes?
9. How many different brands of plain potato chips are there? For each brand, what is the price of a seven-ounce bag of plain potato chips?
10. Describe two things about this store that you think are special.

Group C: Find three fast-food restaurants in your area. For each restaurant, find the following information:

1. Name of restaurant.
2. Location of restaurant.
3. Restaurant hours.
4. Main kind of food (hamburgers, pizza, and so on).
5. Can customers eat in the restaurant? If yes, is there table service?
6. Does the restaurant have a drive-through window?
7. Does the restaurant offer any specials? If so, describe what they include and how much they cost.
8. What is the most expensive item on the menu?
9. How many different kinds of beverages are served? What are they?
10. Describe two things about this restaurant that you think are special.

Group D: Find three stores that sell appliances or electronic equipment. For each store, find the following information:

1. Name of store.
2. Location of store.
3. Store hours.
4. Return policy.
5. Does the store accept credit cards? If so, which ones?
6. Can customers pay in installments for large items ?
7. What is the size of the largest TV that the store sells? What is the brand? How much does it cost?
8. What is the size of the smallest TV that the store sells? What is the brand? How much does it cost?
9. What is the price of a 20-inch Sony TV? What features does it have?
10. Describe two things about this store that you think are special.

Group E: Find three stores that sell books. For each store, find the following information:

1. Name of store.
2. Location of store.
3. Store hours.
4. Return policy.
5. Does the store accept credit cards? If so, which ones?
6. Does the store sell used books?
7. Does the store sell other items besides books? If so, what are these items?
8. What is the price of a paperback copy of *The American Heritage Dictionary*?
9. Which section in this store has the most books?
10. Describe two things about this store that you think are special.

CHAPTER SIX

Community Services: "A Tight Balancing Act"

Part I   Pre-listening: Credit Card Bills

Exercise 1   **Directions:** With a partner, study this bill to answer the questions on page 72:

ACCOUNT NUMBER 6498-3718-9127-5534	GONIF-CARD *Statement* Name William/Irene Baker			GONIF-CARD Center ◄ SEND BILLING INQUIRES TO P.O. Box 9785 Portland, OR 97217		

Closing Date 09-30-95	Credit Limit 5700	Unused Credit 5544	New Balance 155|90	Member Since 07/82 N	24-hour Customer Service 1-800-555-7865

POSTING MO. DAY	REFERENCE NUMBERS	ACTIVITY SINCE LAST STATEMENT		TRANSACTION DATE IF AVAILABLE	CHARGES	PAYMENTS AND CREDITS
0815	98705624	Payment--Thank you				264|97
0824	50522987	Power Records	Portland OR	0820	35|30	
0828	98709956	Smith's Electrics	Portland OR	0825	22|35	
0910	34919824	Redbone General Store	Beaverton OR	0907	43|25	
0915	86926540	Notell Motel	Ashland OR	0914	55|00	

Previous Balance	Less Payments	Less Credits	Activity	Total FINANCE CHARGE	Other Charges	New Balance
264|97	264|97	.00	Advances .00 Purchases 155|90	.00	.00	155|90

Finance Charge Information	Advances	Purchases	Payment Information	
Average Daily Balance (ABD)	.00	.00	Amount Over Limit	.00
Periodic FINANCE CHARGE on ABD	.00	.00	Amount Past Due	.00
Transaction FINANCE CHARGE	.00	.00	Current Due	16.00
Total FINANCE CHARGE	.00	.00	Minimum Periodic	
Monthly Periodic FINANCE CHARGE Rate	1.417%	1.417%	Payment Due	16.00
Corresponding ANNUAL PERCENTAGE RATE	17.00%	17.00%	Date Payment	
ANNUAL PERCENTAGE RATE	17.00%	17.00%	Due	10-15-95

See Reverse Side For Important Information About Your Account

Credit Card Bill

1. What kind of bill is this?
2. Who received the bill?
3. What is the account number?
4. How many charges are on the bill?
5. How much money do they owe (new balance)?
6. What is the minimum amount they can pay (minimum periodic payment due)?
7. What is their credit limit?
8. How much unused credit do they still have?
9. What is the corresponding annual percentage rate?
10. Do the Bakers have to pay a finance charge?
11. When is payment due?
12. Where did they spend $43.25?
13. On what date did they buy something at Power Records?
14. If this bill is incorrect, what should they do?

Part II Main Dialogue

Exercise 1

Directions: Listen to the dialogue and try to get the general idea of what is happening. Remember, you don't need to understand everything. Just try to think about the following questions:

- Where do you think this dialogue is taking place?
- Do you think these people are rich, middle-class, or poor?
- How does this conversation sound to you: Happy? Serious? Funny? And so on.
- What city do you think they live in?

Exercise 2

rewind

Directions: Now listen to the dialogue again to answer these questions:

1. In which season of the year does this dialogue take place?
2. When does this dialogue probably take place: at the beginning, middle, or end of the month? Why do you think so?
3. Which bill had a mistake on it?
4. Why don't Reenie and Will pay 100 percent of the credit card bill?
5. Why are they trying to save money?
6. Why can't they mail their bill payments right away?

rewind

Directions: Listen to the dialogue one more time. This time listen for the amount of money Reenie and Will need to pay for each bill. Then write the amount in Reenie and Will's bank book. After you have finished, do the arithmetic and find Reenie and Will's current balance.

Date	Check number	Transaction	Amount paid		Amount of deposit		Balance	
							$1,453	29
3/26	305	Gonif Card International					-	
CURRENT BALANCE								

Reenie and Will's Bank Book

Exercise 4

Directions: Listen to these sentences from the dialogue and circle the answer that has the same meaning.

1. (a) How much do I have to pay?

   (b) What mistake did they make?

2. (a) We are wasting money on interest.

   (b) Our interest rates are going down.

3. (a) We should call less during the busy hours of the day.

   (b) We should call more during the busy hours of the day.

4. (a) He might make us move.

   (b) He might start bothering us.

5. (a) We can start planning for our trip.

   (b) We can start saving money for our trip.

6. (a) We don't want the creditors to bother us.

   (b) We don't want the creditors to forget us.

Part III   Expansion

Section 1
Using the Library

Read the following passage with your instructor and discuss the meaning.

In addition to books, libraries contain many materials for the public's pleasure and information. A library is a good place to go when you need information about almost any subject. The people who work in libraries are called *librarians*. Librarians enjoy helping people find whatever they need and welcome any and all questions.

A library provides a quiet space for people to study, read, or glance through picture books or *periodicals* (newspapers and magazines). A library also has *reference materials* (maps, charts, encyclopedias, dictionaries, atlases, and so on) that you can use in the library. You can check out most books, videos, and sound recordings from the library, but you cannot check out reference materials.

In order to find a book or other materials, you need to use the *on-line catalog* (a computer system listing all of the materials that a library has) to search for them. You can search for materials by looking them up under three major headings: subject, author, or title. When you use the on-line catalog, it is important that you first decide what kind of search you want to do.

If you need a book about fishing, for example, you can look for it under the subject *fishing*.

If you know that a particular book about fishing is written by Karen Saginor, you can look it up under the author's name. In American libraries, authors are always listed last name first. To find the book by Karen Saginor, you would type in *Saginor, Karen* in the on-line catalog.

If you know that the title of the book is *Fishing without Flies*, you can look it up under the title.

When you use the on-line catalog to find a book you want, you will need to write down the *call number*, the special number that each library book has. A call number is like an address to tell you where you can find the book in the *stacks*, the library book shelves. You can see the call number for each book on the side of the book. Libraries use one of two systems for numbering their books: the *Dewey decimal system* or the *Library of Congress system*. The Dewey decimal system is used in most public libraries. The Library of Congress system is used in most college libraries. Both systems use a combination of letters and numbers to give each book an address.

After you find the call number for your book, you are ready to look for it in the stacks. It is as easy to look for materials in the library as it is to look for a street number.

Exercise 1A

Directions: Match the word on the left with the definition on the right.

a. call number

b. on-line catalog

c. stacks

d. Library of Congress and Dewey decimal

e. librarian

f. reference materials

g. periodicals

h. subject, author, and title headings

1. The person who helps you in a library

2. The systems of numbering materials in the library

3. The number used to find a book

4. Major ways materials are listed in the on-line catalog

5. Newspapers and magazines

6. Things you cannot take home from a library

7. The bookshelves in the library

8. The computer system that contains important information about all the books

Exercise 1B

Directions: What kind of on-line catalog search (author, title, or subject) would you need to do to find the following material? Circle the correct answer.

a. *The Catcher in the Rye*   AUTHOR   TITLE   SUBJECT

b. Capote, Truman   AUTHOR   TITLE   SUBJECT

c. Volleyball   AUTHOR   TITLE   SUBJECT

d. Wouk, Herman   AUTHOR   TITLE   SUBJECT

e. Nuclear physics   AUTHOR   TITLE   SUBJECT

f. *Death Be Not Proud*   AUTHOR   TITLE   SUBJECT

Exercise 1C

Directions: With a partner, study the map of a typical branch library on page 76 and answer the following questions:

1. Where would you go to find the location of a book about sports?

2. Where would you go to find the definition of a new word?

3. Where would you go to check out a book?

4. Where would you go to find a large colored map of your country?

5. Where would you go to find today's newspaper?

6. Where would you go to find a book that is very easy to read?

7. Where would you go if you couldn't find the book or information that you were looking for?

8. Where would you go to photocopy something?

9. Look at the fiction section. How are the books arranged in the fiction stacks?

10. Where would you go to find a book of fiction by Mark Twain? (There are two answers.)

Exercise 1D   **Directions:** Listen to the following conversations. After each conversation, write the number of the conversation next to the correct place on the map of the library.

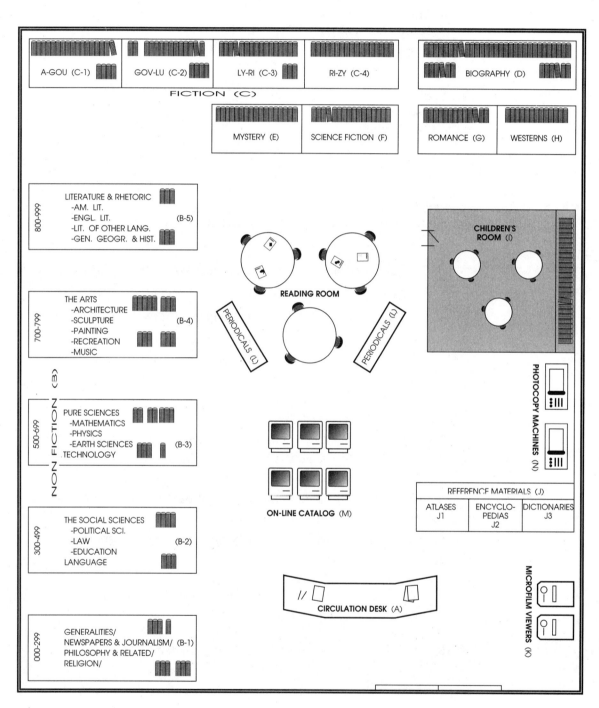

Map of a Typical Branch Library

Section 2

Using the Post Office

Exercise 2A   **Directions:** In pairs or small groups, look at the postal forms on pages 77–79 and answer the following questions:

1. Where can you get the forms?

2. Have you ever used any of the forms? If so, tell your group when and how you used them.

3. What other kinds of forms and items are available at the local post office in your community? Discuss with your group how and why they are used.

4. What are the hours at your local post office? Is there a twenty-four-hour post office in your community?

5. How much does it cost to send a letter in this country? How much does it cost to send a postcard in this country? How much does it cost to send letters and postcards from this country to your native country? Is the weight of the letter important? If yes, how is it important?

6. What is an aerogramme? How much does it cost and how do you use one?

7. What is *junk mail*? What kinds of junk mail do you get?

8. On what days is there no mail delivery?

```
· IMPORTANT:   Present this form to obtain your mail.      ARTICLE NO.
                ID required. Signature may be required.

You may pick up your mail after _____ M. (Date)_____    MAIL
                                                              IS    ▶
_____ or notify your carrier or Post Office for redelivery.  AT

☐ Registered   ☐ Numbered    ☐ Custom (Omit Number)    ☐ Letter  ☐ Flat
                  Insured       Rtn Rcpt      Postage
☐ Certified    ☐COD            ☐ for Mdse    ☐ Due       ☐ Parcel  ☐ Hold

☐ Special | For special      ☐ Placed Under Your Door.   ☐ Restricted
  Delivery| deliveries: Article ☐ Placed in Your Letter Box.  Delivery
☐ If not called for at Post Office before carrier begins
  his next regular trip he will deliver it to you.          ZIP of Origin

Final Notice              Return Date           Amount Due
                                                $

Customer (Please describe    Address Name (Print)
any visible damage)
                             Address


Delivered by and Date     Received By
                          X

PS Form 3849, Mar. 1988    DELIVERY NOTICE/REMINDER/RECEIPT
```

Station "C" 285-7382
1198 So. Van Ness Ave. 94110-9991
9:00 AM to 5:30 PM, Mon. - Fri.
8:30 AM to 3:00 PM, Sat.
Thank you, we appreciate your business.

Left With Residential Unit Manager

Form A

```
CUSTOMS—DOUANE C 1

May be Officially Opened
(Peut être ouvert d'office)
_____
SEE INSTRUCTIONS ON BACK
Contents in detail:
Désignation détaillée
du contenu: _____

_____
_____
_____
_____

Mark X here if a gift . . . . . . . ( )
Il s'agit d'un cadeau

or a sample of merchandise . . . . . ( )
d'un échantillon de marchandises

Value: _____  Weight: _____
Valeur             Poids
PS Form 2976, Feb. 1989
```

Form B

```
                              Rt. No._____ Hold No.___

AUTHORIZATION TO HOLD MAIL  (30 Day Maximum)

It is understood that I will pick up all mail on hand before
delivery is resumed.
    NAME: (Print)  _____
    ADDRESS:       _____
    SIGNATURE:     _____

DATE: From _____ To: Until Pick Up
```

Clerk: ENTER	Carrier: ENTER	Clerk: CANCEL	Carrier: CANCEL
DATE_____	DATE_____	DATE_____	DATE_____
INITIAL___	INITIAL___	INITIAL___	INITIAL___

Form C

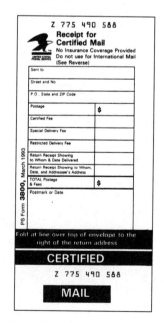

Form D

Form E

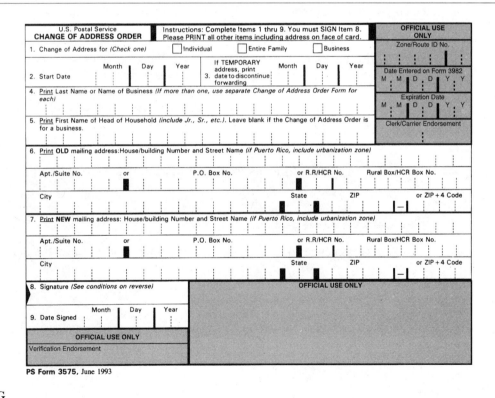

POST OFFICE TO ADDRESSEE EXPRESS MAIL   EF 572084499US

MAILING COPY

ORIGIN (POSTAL USE ONLY)

INTERNATIONAL SHIPMENTS ONLY	P.O. ZIP	Day of Delivery ☐ Next ☐ Second	☐ Flat Rate Envelope
☐ Business Papers	Date In Mo. Day Yr.	☐ 12 Noon ☐ 3 PM	Postage $
☐ Merchandise	Time In ☐ AM. ☐ PM.	Military ☐ 2nd Day ☐ 3rd Day	Return Receipt C.O.D.
Customs forms and commercial invoice may be required. See Pub 273 and International Mail Manual	Weight lbs oz	Int'l Alpha Country Code	Total Postage & Fees
	No Delivery ☐ Weekend ☐ Holiday	Acceptance Clerk Initials	$

DELIVERY (POSTAL USE ONLY)

Delivery Attempt Mo. Day	Time ☐ AM ☐ PM	Employee Signature
Delivery Attempt Mo. Day	Time ☐ AM ☐ PM	Employee Signature
Delivery Attempt Mo. Day	Time ☐ AM ☐ PM	Employee Signature

Signature of Adressee or Agent
X

Name - Please Print
X

CUSTOMER USE ONLY

METHOD OF PAYMENT:

Express Mail Corporate Acct. No.

Federal Agency Acct. No. or Postal Service Acct. No.

☐ WAIVER OF SIGNATURE (Domestic Only): I wish delivery to be made without obtaining the signature of the addressee or the addressee's agent (if in the judgement of the delivery employee, the article can be left in a secure location) and I authorize the delivery employee to sign that the shipment was delivered and understand that the signature of the delivery employee will constitute valid proof of delivery.

NO DELIVERY
☐ WEEKEND ☐ HOLIDAY   Customer Signature

FROM: (PLEASE PRINT)   PHONE _____

TO: (PLEASE PRINT)   PHONE _____

PLEASE PRESS HARD   YOU ARE MAKING 3 COPIES

For Pickup or Tracking Call 1-800-222-1811

Form F

| U.S. Postal Service **CHANGE OF ADDRESS ORDER** | Instructions: Complete Items 1 thru 9. You must SIGN Item 8. Please PRINT all other items including address on face of card. | **OFFICIAL USE ONLY** |

1. Change of Address for (Check one) ☐ Individual ☐ Entire Family ☐ Business

Zone/Route ID No.

2. Start Date   Month Day Year

If TEMPORARY address, print date to discontinue forwarding   Month Day Year

Date Entered on Form 3982 M M D D Y Y

4. Print Last Name or Name of Business (If more than one, use separate Change of Address Order Form for each)

Expiration Date M M D D Y Y

5. Print First Name of Head of Household (include Jr., Sr., etc.). Leave blank if the Change of Address Order is for a business.

Clerk/Carrier Endorsement

6. Print OLD mailing address: House/building Number and Street Name (if Puerto Rico, include urbanization zone)

Apt./Suite No.   or   P.O. Box No.   or R.R/HCR No.   Rural Box/HCR Box No.

City   State   ZIP   or ZIP + 4 Code

7. Print NEW mailing address: House/building Number and Street Name (if Puerto Rico, include urbanization zone)

Apt./Suite No.   or   P.O. Box No.   or R.R/HCR No.   Rural Box/HCR Box No.

City   State   ZIP   or ZIP + 4 Code

8. Signature (See conditions on reverse)

OFFICIAL USE ONLY

9. Date Signed   Month Day Year

OFFICIAL USE ONLY

Verification Endorsement

PS Form 3575, June 1993

Form G

Exercise 2B   **Directions:** Look at the post office forms again and listen to the following people explain which services they need. Then, match the correct form to each person. Write your answers in the blanks.

Example   *Form A*

1. _____

2. _____

3. _____

4. _____

5. _____

6. _____

Part IV   Focus: Active versus Passive Forms

Active and Passive Verbs

You have already studied active and passive verb forms in English. For example, you know that if you hear the active verb sentence: "The Internal Revenue Service sent Gina a check," the Internal Revenue Service is doing the action (sending the check) and Gina is receiving the action (getting the check).

You also know that if you hear the passive sentence: "Gina was sent the check by the Internal Revenue Service," the Internal Revenue Service is again doing the action and Gina is again receiving the action.

In active sentences, the subject of the sentence is the doer of the action.
In passive sentences, the subject of the sentence is the receiver or the object of the doer's action.

To become better listeners, you need to be able to recognize a passive sentence. Passive sentences are signaled by:

BE + PAST PARTICIPLE + (BY + THE REAL DOER OF THE ACTION)

Passive sentences only sometimes end with *by* followed by the doer of the action.

Example   Mr. Johnson's mail <u>is</u> <u>delivered</u> at 11:00 A.M. every day (by the mail carrier).

That book <u>was</u> <u>returned</u> six days late (by my lazy classmate).

The cafeteria <u>is being</u> <u>remodeled</u> this semester (by the construction workers).

Exercise 1

Directions: Listen to the following sentences. For each sentence, circle the correct form of the verb that you hear.

1. Active	Passive	**5.** Active	Passive
2. Active	Passive	**6.** Active	Passive
3. Active	Passive	**7.** Active	Passive
4. Active	Passive	**8.** Active	Passive

Exercise 2

Directions: Listen to the following sentences. For each sentence that you hear, decide who the doer of the action is. Circle the correct answer.

Example   (a) The phone company

(b) Mark

1. (a) The local grocery

   (b) Customers

2. (a) The fire department

   (b) The building

3. (a) The university

   (b) We don't know

4. (a) Kitty

   (b) A bank

5. (a) People

   (b) Water

6. (a) Mr. Lopez

   (b) Louisa

7. (a) Edward

   (b) His brother

8. (a) Alice's car

   (b) The police

Active and Passive Adjectives

Many adjectives come from verbs and are either active or passive. Let's take a look at how active and passive adjectives are made.

DOER VERSUS RECEIVER

Active Adjectives for the Doer

Active adjectives describe the doer of the action.

Example   <u>The credit card bill</u> <u>confused</u> Will and Reenie.

The credit card bill did something: it confused. If we want to describe the bill and its action, we use *confusing*: the active (present participle "-ing") adjective.

The credit card bill was *confusing*.
or
It was a *confusing* bill.

Passive Adjectives for the Receiver

Passive adjectives describe the receiver of an action.

Example   <u>Will and Reenie</u> <u>were confused</u> by the credit card bill.

Will and Reenie received something: they received confusion. If we want to describe Will and Reenie and what they received, we use *confused*: the passive (past participle "-ed") adjective.

Will and Reenie were *confused*.

CONTINUING VERSUS COMPLETED ACTION

Active Adjectives for Continuing Action

Active adjectives (present participles) can also show that an action is still taking place.

Example   The child ran in front of the *stopping* car.
(The car was still moving when the child ran in front of it.)

Passive Adjectives for Continuing Action

Passive adjectives (past participles) can also show that an action has been completed.

Example   The child ran in front of the *stopped* car.
(The car was no longer moving when the child ran in front of it.)

Exercise 3

Directions: Listen to the following sentences and circle the sentence with the same meaning.

Example   **(a)** Rodney was confusing.

⊙**(b)** Rodney was confused.

1. **(a)** The students were annoyed.
   (b) The students were annoying.

2. **(a)** Martha was embarrassed.
   (b) Martha was embarrassing.

3. **(a)** Theresa's grade was disappointing.
   (b) Theresa's grade was disappointed.

4. **(a)** The students are bored.
   (b) The students are boring.

5. **(a)** Sandy was shocking.
   (b) Sandy was shocked.

Exercise 4

Directions: Listen to the following sentences. Then, circle the sentence with the same meaning.

Example   **(a)** The teacher didn't understand.

⊙**(b)** The students didn't understand.

1. **(a)** My neighbor scares me.
   (b) My neighbor is afraid.

2. **(a)** Donna thinks she likes him.
   (b) Donna thinks he likes her.

3. **(a)** The books were in the air.
   (b) The books were on the floor.

4. **(a)** Their son is still a child.
   (b) Their son is an adult.

5. **(a)** They are still married.
   (b) They are not married.

Part V   Listening Practice

Exercise 1

Directions: You will hear eight questions. Read the three possible responses and circle the correct answer.

1. (a) Fill out a change of address form.

    (b) Fill out a mail hold form.

    (c) Fill out an express mail form.

2. (a) In two weeks.

    (b) Fifty cents a day.

    (c) Check the on-line catalogue.

3. (a) Your last payment was five days late.

    (b) You paid five dollars too much last month.

    (c) Yes, that's right. It's five dollars.

4. (a) Nothing this month.

    (b) That's 18 percent a year.

    (c) $2,500-credit limit.

5. (a) That depends on the destination.

    (b) It will take two days to deliver.

    (c) You must fill out a custom's form.

6. (a) In the fiction section.

    (b) In the periodical section.

    (c) In the reference section.

7. (a) Just dial 411.

    (b) Yes, they are free.

    (c) Four each month.

8. (a) $15 per unit.

    (b) Go to the registration office.

    (c) You have to take a test.

Exercise 2   **Directions:** You will hear eight sentences. Read the three choices and circle the correct answer.

1. (a) The person's credit limit is $2,600.

    (b) The person's unused credit is $400.

    (c) The person charged $3,000.

2. (a) You must mail the package after 3 P.M.

    (b) The package will arrive before 10 A.M.

    (c) You must mail the package before 10 A.M.

3. (a) Both are free.

    (b) Only the library is free.

    (c) Only the recycling center is free.

4. (a) You can check out the almanac.

    (b) An almanac is a reference book.

    (c) An almanac is a periodical.

5. (a) December's bill was $30.

    (b) December's bill was $60.

    (c) January's bill wasn't $13.

6. (a) Blossomdale's was high.

    (b) Both were high.

    (c) Cottonworth's was high.

7. (a) I was not nice.

    (b) Mary wasn't nice.

    (c) The operator wasn't nice.

8. (a) Susan was not interested.

    (b) Susan was not interesting.

    (c) Her friends were interested.

Exercise 3

Directions: Listen to the conversation. Each time you hear the bell, circle the sentence that you think is correct.

1. **(a)** This person needs a checking account.

   (b) This person needs a savings account.

2. **(a)** This person should open an interest-bearing checking account.

   (b) This person should not open an interest-bearing checking account.

3. **(a)** This person should open a special bonus savings account.

   (b) This person should not open a special bonus savings account.

4. **(a)** This person is going to open a special bonus savings account.

   (b) This person is not going to open a special bonus savings account.

5. **(a)** This person should open an interest-bearing checking account.

   (b) This person should open a special bonus savings account.

   (c) This person should open a regular savings account.

Exercise 4

Directions: You will hear two conversations. At the beginning of each conversation you will hear a question. Listen to the conversation. Then, circle the best answer.

1. **(a)** June

   (b) December

   (c) April

2. **(a)** Certified-return receipt

   (b) First-class priority

   (c) Express mail

Part VI   Using It: Planning a Community of the Future

It is the year 2100. Space travel is very common, and it is time to plan the first community to live on another planet. As a class, decide on which planet you would like to build a new community. Decide how your planet is similar to and different from Earth. Choose a name for your new community.

Exercise

Directions: For this exercise you'll discuss specific services for your new community. After your instructor has divided the class into groups, follow the instructions below for your group only. You'll need to use your imagination to come up with ideas showing the changes you think will happen by the year 2100. After you have completed the exercise, share your information with the rest of the class in order to get a complete picture of how your new community might look.

Group A: Transportation What kind of vehicles will there be on your planet and who will be allowed to drive them? Will there be an age limit for getting a driver's license? Will there be a fee to get a license? Will vehicle insurance be required? What kind of public transportation will be available in your community? Where will the spaceship port be? How often will public transportation vehicles run? What kind of conveniences will there be in public transportation vehicles? (For example, will there be mini TVs in the vehicles?) Think of anything else you would like to add to make transportation easy, comfortable, and safe in your new community.

Group B: Utilities, Banking, and Postal Services How will people buy things in your community? Will people use cash, or will there be some other way to buy and sell things and services? Will there be banks? If so, what kind of services will they provide? What utilities will your community need? Will gas and electricity be available, or will some other form of power be used? Who will own the utility companies? How will people communicate with one another in your city? Will there be telephones, or will other forms of communication be used? Will there be postal services? If so, how will postal services be different in the year 2100? Think of anything else that will make utility, banking, and postal services efficient and convenient in your new community.

Group C: Schools and Information What kinds of schools will there be in your community? Who will go to school and what will they study? How will the schools be different from today's schools? Which school problems of today will be solved by the year 2100, and which problems, if any, will still exist? How will teachers be different? How will students be different? How will people get news and information in your new community? Will there be libraries? Newspapers? Magazines? Bookstores? If so, how will each of these be different from the way they are today? Think of anything else that will make education and information things that people can easily get in your new community.

Group D: Government What kind of government will there be in your new community? What kind of government leaders will be needed? How will they get their jobs? What kind of police force will there be? What power will police have? Will there be an army? If so, why? Will people have guns or other weapons? How will crime be prevented? What important laws will be needed for your new community? Who will make the laws? What will be illegal in the year 2100 that is legal today? What will be legal in the year 2100 that is illegal today? What will happen when people break the laws? What other important areas of government do you need to think about to make your new community safe and fair for all of its citizens?

Group E: Recreation and Entertainment What kind of open spaces will be available in your new community? What will be special about the open space areas? How will parks and recreation areas be different in the year 2100? What will people do for entertainment in your new community? How will types of entertainment that are popular today be different in the year 2100? What sports will be popular? What kinds of sports centers will your community need to build? Will there be a symphony orchestra, an opera company, or a dance company? If so, where will they perform? Will people still go to movies and watch television? What kinds of museums will there be in your community? What will people do for vacation? How much vacation time will they get? Include any other ideas you have about recreation and entertainment.

CHAPTER SEVEN

Employment:
"First Day on the Job"

Part I   Pre-listening: Job Ads

Exercise 1   **Directions:** In pairs or small groups, read the job advertisements. Circle all the abbreviations and try to guess their meanings. Then, discuss the ads with your teacher.

Help Wanted

Cashier P/T; eve; must be 18 yrs. of age; exp pref, but will train; appl in per at: S & G Supermarket 940 Filbert Street An Equal Opportunity Employer	**Mechanic** Min 5 yrs.exp in truck repairs. Must have own tools. Gd. sal. and benefits. Ed: 521-4455
Jobs 'R Us Agency *** 392-1818 *** 100% Free! Specialize in retail and clerical placements. Many temp, perm, and summer positions. Reg, swing, and graveyard shifts. CALL TODAY!	**Secretary** Immed. opening. P/T Flex. hrs. Type 50 WPM, computer knowledge a must. Nonsmoking office. Send résumé to: Barret Grp., P.O. Box 12, Long Beach, CA 90803
Cook Experienced breakfast cook for busy dwntwn rest. Min 2 yrs. exp; local references req. Judy: 671-1213	**Teacher** Bilingual classroom (Eng/Span) exc. salary and benefits. Must have valid credentials. Résumé and letter of interest to Kirkwood Elementary School, P.O. Box 141, Harrison, N.J. 07029

Exercise 2   **Directions:** Read the following descriptions. Decide which job each person should apply for and how each should answer the ad.

1. John Guerrero graduated from high school last month and wants to work for a year to save money for college. He speaks English and Spanish and enjoys working with people.

2. Andrea Martinelli was laid off from her job at Jenson's Auto Fix-It Shop. She wants to find a job that has good medical insurance.

3. Bill Wilkes is a house husband who has been taking care of his children for the last seven years. He wants to go back to work part-time, but he needs to find a job that lets him work different hours every day. He is an excellent typist and owns his own computer.

4. Sarah Billingsly is a retired Spanish teacher. She stopped working three years ago, but she really misses her job and wants to go back to work.

5. Danny Goodson just moved here and needs to find a job. In his hometown he worked as a cook for five years. He wants to find a part-time job at night so he can take classes in the morning.

Part II   Main Dialogue

Exercise 1   **Directions:** Listen to the dialogue and try to get a general idea of what is happening. Remember, you don't need to understand everything. Just try to think about the following questions:

- Where do you think this dialogue is taking place?
- What do you think the place looks like?
- How old do you think the speakers are?
- Think of several words to describe each speaker.

Exercise 2

rewind

Directions: Now, listen to the dialogue again to answer these questions:

1. What is Mark's new job?
2. What does Gloria tell Mark about?
3. How long does Mark plan to work at his job? Why?
4. How does Gloria feel about her job? Why?
5. What is Carson's Canine Cuisine?
6. Why does Gloria make a strange sound at the end of the dialogue?

Exercise 3

rewind

Directions: Listen to the dialogue one more time. Then, fill in the chart with any information that you can.

Starting time:	
Ending time:	
Vacation:	
Break time:	
Overtime:	
lunch time:	
Dental plan:	
Retirement plan:	
Union:	
Medical insurance:	

Exercise 4:

Directions: Listen to these sentences from the dialogue and circle the answer that has the same meaning.

1. **(a)** I'll be driving the delivery trucks.

   (b) I'll be putting boxes into the delivery trucks.

2. **(a)** I wanted to know about all the jobs in the dog food business.

   (b) I wanted to have the easiest job in the dog food business.

3. **(a)** That would make me crazy.

   (b) That would make me sad.

4. **(a)** You really look very young.

   (b) I really think you started only five years ago.

5. **(a)** You'll change your mind.

   (b) You'll learn new songs.

6. **(a)** He likes dog food a lot.

   (b) His father is the owner of the company.

Exercise 5

Directions: How does Gloria feel at the end of the dialogue? What do you think will happen next? Will it be a good ending or a bad ending? On a separate piece of paper, finish the conversation between Gloria, Mark, and Mr. Carson.

Part III   Expansion: Career Choices—Interest Inventory

Exercise 1   **Directions:** Read the following passage. Circle any words you do not know, and try to guess their meanings. Discuss the information with your instructor. Then, answer the questions that follow.

People in the United States and Canada are free to choose the kind of work they do. While it is not always easy for people to get their first job choice, they are taught to prepare for the jobs they are interested in by getting correct training and education. In high school and college, there are special counselors who help students plan their job futures. The government also has special counselors who can help people who are no longer in school. We call these counselors *career counselors.*

Your *career* is the specific kind of work you have chosen and trained for. When you choose and plan your career, you are using your freedom of choice which is part of the American Dream. The average North American not only chooses a career, but also has the chance to change careers if he or she later becomes interested in a different kind of job. This is not unusual at all, and people of all ages (from twenty through sixty and older) often return to community colleges, vocational training programs, and universities to learn new skills and make career changes.

1. Did you choose your current or previous job?
2. Did you train for your current or previous job?
3. Did you train for another kind of job?
4. Is it common for adults in your country to change careers?

Exercise 2A   **Directions:** You are now going to play a game. You will dream about the kind of job you would *love* to have. Forget about money. Forget about your English level. Forget about what your family would like you to do. This is a game! Try to be honest. You will find the perfect career of your dreams.

Look at the following list of job skills. For each group, circle the skill you are most interested in. Choose only *one* skill for each group.

1. **(a)** Studying something very carefully (observing)

    (b) Using your hands to do things (handling)

    (c) Listening and talking to others (communicating)

2. **(a)** Exercising or using your body to do things (being athletic)

    (b) Giving or following directions (cooperating)

    (c) Finding out how things are different or the same (comparing)

3. **(a)** Copying, making lists and keeping records (recording)

    (b) Making others happy or helping others (performing and serving)

    (c) Working outdoors (working with the earth)

4. **(a)** Working in pairs or groups (sharing)

    (b) Using machines and vehicles (being mechanical)

    (c) Looking at things very carefully to find out about them or deciding what is good and bad (analyzing and evaluating)

5. **(a)** Working with numbers (computing)

(b) Fixing things (repairing)

(c) Showing others how to do things or training others (leading)

6. **(a)** Changing peoples' ideas and opinions (persuading)

(b) Putting things into groups (organizing)

(c) Using tools (manipulating things)

7. **(a)** Building things (constructing)

(b) Thinking of new ideas and planning ways to do things (planning and developing)

(c) Giving advice to others (advising)

Exercise 2B   **Directions:** The skills you are studying can be put into three categories: skills for working with people, skills for using *information*, and *physical* skills involving the use of the body or things. Go back over the skills listed in the previous exercise and decide which category each skill belongs in. Write each skill in the correct column below and circle the skills you chose as your answers in Exercise 1. The first one has been done for you.

PEOPLE	*INFORMATION*	*PHYSICAL*
communicating	observing	handling

Count the number of skills you circled in each category and write down the totals:

Total *People* skills: _____

Total *Information* skills: _____

Total *Physical* skills: _____

Total number of skills should equal: ____7____

Divide into small groups and discuss your choices. Fill in the table below with jobs that use people, information, and physical skills. The first few have been done for you. Try to find a job that uses all three skill areas equally.

People skills	Information skills	Physical skills
teacher	teacher	mechanic
	accountant	

Exercise 2C **Directions:** In groups, discuss and answer these questions:

1. Make a list of as many work environments as you can think of, such as outdoors, in an office, in a factory, and so on.
2. If you could choose between a job that you didn't like but that paid a high salary and a job that you liked a lot but that paid a low salary, which job would you choose? Why?
3. What is your preferred work schedule?
4. What is your dream job?
5. Do you need people, information, or physical skills for this job?
6. What other, specific skills do you need for this job?
7. Will you need special training, a college degree, or a specific certificate for this job?

Exercise 3A

Directions: Ted is having a conversation with a career counselor. He is looking for a job but is having trouble deciding what kind of job to look for. Listen to the conversation and circle the correct information on the chart.

Skill area (Circle one)	People Information Things
Specific skills (Circle the correct one(s))	Organizing Repairing Analyzing Computing
Job experiences (Circle the correct one(s))	Refrigerator repairman Moving man Salesman Bus driver
Time preference (Circle one)	9–5 Any shift Part-time
Advancement (Circle one)	Important Not important
Salary (Circle one)	High Not important
Location preferred (Circle one)	Inside Outdoors At home Traveling

What new job do you think would be good for Ted? _____

Exercise 3B

Directions: Now listen to the job counselor's suggestions for Ted and two other people. First, write the job that you think the counselor recommends for each person. Then, circle the job that you think the counselor has recommended for Ted. Write down any words that help you guess the jobs.

Job 1. _____

Job 2. _____

Job 3. _____

Part IV Focus: Intonation of Statements

Falling Intonation

North American speakers of English use *falling intonation* to make most declarative statements; that is, the voice drops at the end of a sentence that makes a simple statement of truth or fact.

Examples   I'll be loading the delivery trucks.

              I'm a business student.

              He's just like his father.

      Falling intonation in a statement indicates that the statement is complete in the speaker's mind. The statement does not depend on any other information to be complete. The speaker is *sure* of the statement and is not asking for confirmation from the listener.

Rising Intonation

When we use *rising intonation* in a statement (that is, when the voice goes up at the end of a sentence), we show that we are not completely sure of the information and that we need the listener to confirm that we are making a statement that is true. In other words, we turn the statement into a kind of yes/no question.

Examples   You're still in college?   Yes, I'm a business student.

              You've been working a long time?   Uh huh . . . fifteen years.

              Quarter to eight?   Yes, that's what I said.

      Notice that in writing, these statements indicate that they are really yes/no questions by using question marks (?). For each one, the listener needs to answer either *yes* or *no*.

      If these same statements are spoken with falling intonation they become simple statements of truth or fact. The listener does not need to confirm the information. The listener will probably make another statement to keep the conversation going.

Examples   You're still in college.   Don't worry. I'll be a good worker.

              You've been working a long time.   You're right. I really need a vacation.

              Quarter to eight.   I'll remember that.

Rising intonation in statements can also show surprise or shock. When we are surprised or shocked by information that seems unbelievable, we check to see if we have the correct information. Statements of surprise or shock are very much like yes/no questions.

Examples   Fifteen years? ↗   Yes, that's what I said.

His father, sir? ↗   Why yes, of course.

When you hear rising intonation in a statement, you know that the speaker needs more information or confirmation. Even if you don't understand every word the speaker says, your knowledge of rising intonation in statements will help you understand that the speaker needs an answer.

Exercise 1

Directions: Listen to the following sentences and decide whether each sentence uses rising (↗) or falling (↘) intonation. Circle the correct answer.

Example   Rising (↗) Falling (↘)

1. (↗)   (↘)
2. (↗)   (↘)
3. (↗)   (↘)
4. (↗)   (↘)
5. (↗)   (↘)
6. (↗)   (↘)
7. (↗)   (↘)
8. (↗)   (↘)
9. (↗)   (↘)
10. (↗)   (↘)

Directions: Now listen to these same sentences. Pay close attention to the rising or falling intonation. After you hear each sentence, circle the best response.

Example   **(a)** Yes, $1,000,000—tax free.

           (b) Oh my God. I'm so happy.*

1.   **(a)** Yes, that's the right time.

     (b) Oh, that's too early.

2.   **(a)** That's right. You don't have to pay.

     (b) This is much better than the plan at my old job.

3.   **(a)** No, nothing at all.

     (b) I don't think I want to work here.

4.   **(a)** Yes, I'll give you her phone number.

     (b) Good. I really need to talk to someone.

5.   **(a)** Yes. I want you to stay until 10:00.

     (b) That's too bad. Now we can't go to the movies.

6.   **(a)** Of course. It's for a children's doctor.

     (b) Maybe Dr. Smith should answer the ad.

7.   **(a)** Yes. All workers must belong to the union.

     (b) O.K. That's not a problem for me.

8.   **(a)** That's not fair.

     (b) No, they get $3.00 less!

9.   **(a)** That's terrible. I feel sorry for her.

     (b) Yes, she came two hours late.

10.   **(a)** Thank you. I'll wait until he is ready.

     (b) Yes, Mr. Baily is his name.

* The correct answer is *a* because the speaker used rising intonation which indicated a yes/no question. Therefore the answer with *yes* is the correct response.

Part V   Listening Practice

Exercise 1

Directions: You will hear eight sentences. Read the three possible responses and circle the correct answer.

1. (a) No, it's not a full-time job.

    (b) I make $10.80 an hour.

    (c) Usually between three and four.

2. (a) I can start immediately.

    (b) I have two years experience.

    (c) I don't mind working overtime.

3. (a) No, you need to be a college graduate.

    (b) Yes, you need many local references.

    (c) Yes, and you also need a state certificate.

4. (a) Yes, the boss is very nice.

    (b) Oh good. I need to pick my son up.

    (c) No, that's only if you work overtime.

5. (a) I don't want to work on Saturdays.

    (b) Both of them.

    (c) I need to send them a résumé.

6. (a) I read about the job in the newspaper ad.

    (b) I'm going to take a typing class next semester.

    (c) I worked in a department store for four years.

7. (a) I want to spend time with my kids during the day.

    (b) I want to take some computer classes at night.

    (c) I want to apply for the night job.

8. (a) There's at least one day of overtime a week.

    (b) They have a medical, a dental, and a retirement plan.

    (c) You can join the union after six months.

Exercise 2

Directions: You will hear seven sentences. Read the three choices and circle the correct answer.

1. (a) You can get medical insurance right away.

   (b) You can't get medical insurance here.

   (c) You can get medical insurance in half a year.

2. (a) I can work from 9:00 to 5:00 every day.

   (b) I can work forty hours per week.

   (c) I can work four hours per day.

3. (a) Applicants should send a résumé to the company.

   (b) Applicants should go to the company.

   (c) Applicants should call the company.

4. (a) I am really surprised that Mary came late.

   (b) I want you to know that Mary came late.

   (c) I am sad that Mary came late.

5. (a) He has excellent people skills.

   (b) He has excellent physical skills.

   (c) He has excellent information skills.

6. (a) You should start out as the manager.

   (b) You should start out as a cook's assistant.

   (c) You should start out as an owner.

7. (a) I'd like a job that uses people skills.

   (b) I'd like a job that uses information skills.

   (c) I'd like a job that uses physical skills.

Exercise 3

Directions: Listen to the conversation. Each time you hear the bell, circle the sentence that you think is correct.

1. (a) She has a college degree.

   (b) She doesn't have a college degree.

2. (a) She has a college degree.

   (b) She doesn't have a college degree.

3. (a) She is applying for a job as a legal assistant.

   (b) She is applying for a job as a secretary.

4. (a) She is applying for a job as a legal assistant.

   (b) She is applying for a job as a secretary.

5. (a) She has a college degree.

   (b) She doesn't have a college degree.

6. (a) She should be hired.

   (b) She shouldn't be hired.

Exercise 4

Directions: You will hear three conversations. At the beginning of each conversation, you will hear a question. Listen to the conversation. Then, circle the best answer.

1. (a) Auto repair program.

   (b) Real estate program.

   (c) Dental assistant program.

2. (a) They want better medical coverage.

   (b) They want better vacation and sick leave.

   (c) They want better salaries.

3. (a) People skills.

   (b) Information skills.

   (c) Physical skills.

Part VI   Using It: Solving Problems at Work

Exercise 1   **Directions:** With a partner read the following employment problems. For each one, discuss possible solutions.

1. You have been working for the same company for five years. You do a very good job and your boss seems to like you very much. You think that you should get a raise in pay. Your boss would like to give you more money but the company is very small and business is not very good right now.

2. Your union has recommended that your company go on strike to get better pay and health insurance. Your co-worker agrees with the union 100 percent and cannot understand why you are not sure. You have several reasons for feeling that going on strike is a bad idea right now. Your co-worker has good arguments for each of your reasons.

3. You are very unhappy about your job and want to make a change, but you don't know what you want to do. You talk to a job counselor who helps you make a decision.

4. A family member in your home country is sick and you must leave work for three weeks to take care of him or her. Your boss understands the situation but really cannot work without your help.

5. You really like your job and you are very good at it. However, your boss often says things to you that are too personal. He or she talks about your body and asks you many personal questions about your love life. You feel that you are being sexually harassed and you would like your boss to stop.

6. You and your friend have been working together at the same company for six months. You are very good at your job, but your friend is lazy and always asks for help. You are tired of doing your friend's work in addition to yours and you need to talk to your friend about it.

Exercise 2   **Directions:** Choose one of the six employment problems in Exercise 1, a problem from the Main Dialogue, or one of your own. With your partner, role-play the problem. Make sure that you speak to each other for at least two minutes. After you have practiced your role play, present it to the class.

CHAPTER EIGHT

Emergency Services: "Crime in the Street"

Part I   Pre-listening: Headlines

Exercise 1   **Directions:** In pairs or small groups, read and describe what happened in each newspaper headline in the illustration. Then, from the following list, choose words that have the same meaning as the underlined words. Write the new words above the underlined ones. The first one has been done for you as an example.

Arson	Burglarize	Kidnapped	Murdered
Mugged	Raped	Rob	Stolen

Burglarize

Thieves Take $25,000 Painting From Art Museum

1. THREE YOUTHS DIE IN DRIVE-BY SHOOTING

2. WOMAN ATTACKED BY MAN ON SUBWAY TRAIN

3. FOUR ARMED MEN TAKE $100,000 FROM CITY BANK

4. BABY TAKEN FROM HOME WHILE MOTHER VISITS NEIGHBOR

5. Wallet Taken From Tourist's Back Pocket While He Watches July 4th Parade

6. WOMAN SEXUALLY ATTACKED IN DARK PARKING LOT

7. CAUSE OF FIRE: MAN BURNS BUILDING FOR INSURANCE MONEY

Newspaper Headlines

Exercise 2   **Directions:** Look at the illustration of rewritten newspaper headlines and re-write the headlines using the words listed below for the people or person who commits the crime. The first one has been done for you as an example.

Arsonist	Burglars	Kidnapers	Mugger
Murderer	Pickpocket	Rapist	Robbers

Burglars Take $25,000 Painting From Art Museum

1. _____ KILLS THREE YOUTHS IN DRIVE-BY SHOOTING

2. _____ ATTACKS WOMAN ON SUBWAY TRAIN

3. _____ TAKE $100,000 FROM CITY BANK

4. _____ TAKE BABY FROM HOME WHILE MOTHER VISITS NEIGHBOR

5. _____ Takes Wallet From Tourist's Back Pocket While Tourist Watches July 4th Parade

6. _____ ATTACKS WOMAN IN DARK PARKING LOT

7. _____ BURNS BUILDING FOR INSURANCE MONEY

Rewritten Newspaper Headlines

Part II   Main Dialogue

Exercise 1   **Directions:** Listen to the dialogue and try to get a general idea of what is happening. Remember, you don't need to understand everything. Just try to think about the following questions:

- Where do you think this dialogue is taking place?
- Who are the people in the dialogue?
- What do you think they look like?
- Are they inside or outside? Try to form a picture of the scene in your mind. Besides the characters in the dialogue, what do you see?

Exercise 2   **Directions:** Now, listen to the dialogue again to answer these questions:

rewind

1. What kind of crime are they talking about?
2. How many people does the man describe?
3. Who does the man think took his wallet?
4. How does the old woman know that the wallet belonged to the man?
5. Why doesn't the police officer arrest anybody?
6. How does the old woman feel at the end of the dialogue? How does the man feel?

Exercise 3

rewind

Directions: Listen to the dialogue one more time. Then, fill in the chart with information about the suspects.

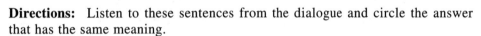

Description	Suspect 1	Suspect 2
Gender (sex)		
Age		
Physical appearance		
Clothing		
Other information		

Exercise 4

Directions: Listen to these sentences from the dialogue and circle the answer that has the same meaning.

1. **(a)** I know that I am 100 percent correct.

   (b) I think that someone tried to kill me.

2. **(a)** Pickpockets like to wear expensive clothes.

   (b) Pickpockets dress so you will not notice them.

3. **(a)** Pickpockets get old quickly.

   (b) Pickpockets can be all ages.

4. **(a)** He looked strange.

   (b) He looked normal.

5. **(a)** If you see his face in our police pictures, we can interview him.

   (b) If you see him mugging someone, we can arrest him.

6. **(a)** Don't call a person a criminal before you are sure.

   (b) Don't call a person a criminal without police help.

Exercise 5   **Directions:** In pairs or small groups discuss the following questions. Ask your teacher for help with any new vocabulary.

1. What is the word for the person who is hurt during any other crime?

2. What is the word for the person who commits any crime?

3. Have you ever been a witness to a crime? If yes, tell your group about the experience.

4. Have you ever been the victim of a crime? If yes, tell your group about the experience.

5. Read the following and decide whether each person is *guilty*, *innocent*, or a *suspect*.

   a. While robbing a bank, Mr. Shephard shoots a bank teller. The police arrest him, and he is sent to jail for thirty years. Mr. Shephard is _____ .

   b. The police are looking for a woman who kidnapped a child. Ms. Jones looks like the kidnaper, so the police bring her to the station to interview her. Ms. Jones is _____ .

   c. Someone told the police that Alan Livingston burned down an empty building on Pine Street. The police find out that Mr. Livingston was in another city the day of the fire. Mr. Livingston is _____ .

6. In most English speaking countries, the law says that if someone is *accused* of a crime, the person is a suspect. The law says that the *accused* person is "innocent until proven guilty." In other words, there must be *proof* that the person committed the crime. Do you think this is a good law? Does your native country have a similar law? List some advantages and some disadvantages of this law.

Part III   Expansion

Section 1
Using 911

Exercise 1A   **Directions:** With a partner, read the list of instructions for using 911 and then answer the questions that follow it. Ask your teacher for help with any new vocabulary.

INSTRUCTIONS FOR USING 911

1. Dial 911 for fire, police, and medical emergencies.
2. In case of an emergency, remain calm. Call the police immediately, not a personal friend or a relative.
3. When the police operator answers, first state your location and the nature of the emergency: "I am at 587 Baker Street and there has just been a robbery here."
4. Remain on the telephone until you are connected with the police radio dispatcher. Answer questions as briefly and accurately as possible.
5. When answering questions, concentrate on describing only one suspect at a time. Always describe suspect from head down to feet.
6. For non-emergency routine police business, call your local police station.

---

1. What is *911*?
2. What is the first thing you should do if you call 911?
3. What does *nature of the emergency* mean?
4. What does *dispatcher* mean?
5. How should you answer the dispatcher's questions?
6. How should you describe suspects?
7. If it is very late at night and your neighbors are making a lot of noise, should you call 911 for help? If not, whom should you call?

Exercise 1B   **Directions:** Listen to the following dialogue between a dispatcher and a person who is calling for help. The person who is calling is not following the instructions for using 911. What is she doing wrong?

_____

_____

_____

Directions: Listen to the dialogue again. Write down all the important information.

rewind

Address			
Crime			
Suspects	Number 1	Number 2	Number 3
Sex			woman
Height/build	tall		✗
Hair		✗	
Clothes		hat	red hooded-sweatshirt, dark sweatpants
Suspect's actions	choking victim		

Exercise 1D

Directions: Now, rewrite the dialogue between the dispatcher and the caller. The caller's response should follow the rules for using 911 in an emergency.

Dispatcher: 911. Emergency assistance.

Caller: _____

_____

_____

Dispatcher: Can you describe the suspects? _____

Caller: _____

_____

_____

Dispatcher: We'll send a police car right away.

Section 2
Disasters

Besides police and medical emergencies, other life-threatening emergencies may involve many members of a community or people in one area of the country. These kinds of emergencies are often the result of natural disasters such as earthquakes, floods, or hurricanes.

Exercise 2A   **Directions:** With a partner or in small groups, describe each of the disasters in the following chart. Talk about things you can do to prepare for each disaster before it occurs. Also, talk about things you should do during the disaster. Finally, discuss what you should do after the disaster. Write your suggestions on the chart.

Disaster Preparedness

Disaster	Before	During	After
Tornado			
Earthquake			
Firestorm			
Flood			
Hurricane or typhoon			
Land or mud slide			
Blizzard			

Directions: Listen to the following conversations to decide what kind of life-threatening disaster the people are talking about. Write your answers in the blanks. Also, write any words that help you.

1. _____

2. _____

3. _____

Part IV   Focus: Time Clauses

In Chapter Five, we studied conjunctions that show contrast and concession. We learned that even if you don't know all of the words in the sentence or clause, you can often guess the meaning from the information that the conjunction gives you.

In this lesson, we will take a look at conjunctions that show time relationships. Listening for these conjunctions will help you understand the time relationship between two actions.

After: Look at the following sentence:

> *After* the movie started, I went to look for my glasses.

There are two actions in this sentence. *After* comes in front of the action that happened first in time. In other words:

> Action 1: The movie started.

> Action 2: I went to look for my glasses.

Before: Look at this sentence using the same two actions as the sentence above:

> *Before* I went to look for my glasses, the movie started.

Before comes in front of the action that happened second in time. In other words:

> Action 1: The movie started.

> Action 2: I went to look for my glasses.

When you hear a sentence with *after* or *before*, remember that *after* comes in front of the action that happened first in time and that *before* comes in front of the action that happened second in time.

Even if you do not understand all of the words in a sentence, *before* and *after* tell you the order of the actions in time.

Directions: Listen to the following clauses and circle the clauses that can be joined to them.

Example   (a)   after the police arrived.

             (b)   before the police arrived.

1. **(a)** before she saw the accident.

    (b) after she saw the accident.

2. **(a)** before he enters a store.

    (b) after he enters a store.

3. **(a)** he took all of the money.

    (b) he quickly drove away.

4. **(a)** after the firefighters made us leave.

    (b) before the firefighters made us leave.

5. **(a)** before the snowstorm became too serious.

    (b) after the snowstorm became too serious.

6. **(a)** before the police arrived.

    (b) after the police arrived.

Exercise 2

Directions: Listen to the following sentences. Then, circle the sentence with the correct meaning.

Example   (a)   First, the police arrested the suspect.

             (b)   First, the police cornered him.

1. **(a)** First he put the receipt in his wallet.

    (b) First, he parked the car.

2. **(a)** First, they called the victim's family.

    (b) First, they called an ambulance.

3. **(a)** First, the dispatcher sent a fire truck.

    (b) First, the dispatcher heard about the fire.

4. **(a)** First, he learned that 3,000 homes were destroyed.

    (b) First, he announced it was a state emergency.

5. **(a)** The electricity went out first.

    (b) The snow was falling first.

6. **(a)** First, the house stopped shaking.

    (b) First, they checked the gas.

Part V   Listening Practice

Directions: You will hear seven questions. Read the three possible responses and circle the correct answer.

1. (a) A tall man wearing a blue jacket.

    (b) 953 Vine Boulevard.

    (c) He's hitting a woman on the head.

2. (a) She was average size and had short black hair.

    (b) She took my purse while I was on the bus.

    (c) It was a large black purse with a leather strap.

3. (a) On the corner of Mayfair and Park Lane South.

    (b) About $150 and a new TV.

    (c) At about 7:30 this evening.

4. (a) A woman was waiting for the robber in his car.

    (b) No, I was alone.

    (c) He took all of my money.

5. (a) Yes, I can.

    (b) Yes, he was.

    (c) He had short red hair.

6. (a) He hit me in the arm two times.

    (b) He had a big gun that he pointed at me.

    (c) He had a big red mark on his chin.

7. (a) Leave your home immediately.

    (b) Stay indoors.

    (c) Go up on your roof.

Exercise 2 **Directions:** You will hear six sentences. Read the three choices and circle the correct answer.

1. (a) First sign the paper. Then describe the suspects.
   (b) First describe the suspects. Then sign the paper.
   (c) If you describe the suspects, sign the paper.

2. (a) Fifty people were killed.
   (b) Thirty-two people were killed.
   (c) Forty people were killed.

3. (a) They stole my TV.
   (b) They stole almost all of my things.
   (c) They stole a cassette player.

4. (a) They need an ambulance.
   (b) They need a police officer.
   (c) They need a mechanic.

5. (a) The pickpocket put his hand in Jan's purse before Jan screamed.
   (b) The pickpocket put his hand in Jan's purse after Jan screamed.
   (c) Before the pickpocket put his hand in Jan's purse, Jan screamed.

6. (a) Mr. Saunders hit someone on the head at 2 P.M.
   (b) Someone hit Mr. Saunders on the head at 2 P.M.
   (c) Someone killed Mr. Saunders.

Exercise 3 **Directions:** Listen to the conversation. Each time you hear the bell, read the statement and circle *True* or *False*.

1. Mr. Smith is probably in trouble with the law.   True   False

2. Mr. Smith is probably in trouble with the law.   True   False

3. Mr. Smith is a murder suspect.   True   False

4. Mr. Smith is a murder suspect.   True   False

Exercise 4 **Directions:** You will hear three conversations. At the beginning of each conversation, you will hear a question. Listen to the conversation. Then, circle the best answer.

1. (a) a murder
   (b) a kidnapping
   (c) a burglary

2. (a) two
   (b) three
   (c) we don't know

3. (a) Man Guilty of Robbery
   (b) Man Innocent of Robbery
   (c) Man Suspected of Robbery

Part VI   Using It: Physical Descriptions

Exercise 1   **Directions:** With your instructor, discuss the police description sheet shown in the figure. Make sure you understand all of the information asked for on the sheet and how the information is used.

DESCRIPTION SHEET

RACE_____SEX _____ AGE _____HEIGHT _____

WEIGHT_____BODY BUILD_____EYES _____

HAIR COLOR _____HAIR TEXTURE_____

COMPLEXION_____SHAPE OF FACE _____

PHYSICAL CHARACTERISTICS: (Describe each one that is applicable)

MANNER OF WALK: _____ SCARS: _____

MARKS:_____TATTOOS: _____GLASSES: _____

MUSTACHE:_____BEARD: _____GOATEE: _____

CLOTHING: (Type and color. Use diagram at left as a guide. Also note any jewelry)

_____

_____

_____

REMARKS: (Note anything unusual about suspect such as accent, manner of speaking, etc.)

_____

_____

Police Description Sheet

Exercise 2   **Directions:** Without telling anyone, select one of your classmates. Use that classmate as a model and fill in the Police Description Sheet in the figure. After everyone has finished, read your description to the rest of the class and have them guess who you are describing.

Health, Fitness, and the Environment: "Kicking the Habit"

Part I   **Pre-listening: Health Survey**

How healthy you are depends on two important things: genetics (what you inherited from your parents) and your own personal lifestyle habits. There is very little you can do about your genetic background, but there is a lot that you can do to develop lifestyle habits that improve your health and fitness.

Exercise 1   **Directions:** Look at the following survey to find out how healthy your lifestyle is. For each section, read each question, and circle the answer that best describes the way you now live. When you have finished each part, write in your total score.

Health Survey

SMOKING
If you never smoked or are an ex-smoker, enter a total score of 10, and move on to the next section.

		YES	*NO*
1.	Do you smoke less than ten cigarettes a day?	1	0
2.	Have you cut down on smoking?	1	0
3.	Do you plan to quit smoking soon?	1	0
4.	Are you trying to quit smoking?	2	0

Your Total Score _____

ALCOHOL AND DRUGS		*FRE-QUENTLY*	*SOME-TIMES*	*ALMOST NEVER*
1.	Do you drink more than two drinks a day?	0	1	2
2.	Do you use alcohol or other drugs to help you relax?	0	1	2
3.	If you drink or use alcohol too much, how often do you try to cut down on your alcohol or drug use? (If you don't drink alcohol or use drugs too much, give yourself 2 points.)	0	1	2

		FRE-QUENTLY	SOME-TIMES	ALMOST NEVER
4.	Do people tell you that you use alcohol or drugs too much?	0	1	2
5.	Do you ever use other people's prescription drugs?	0	1	2

Your Total Score _____

STRESS		FRE-QUENTLY	SOME-TIMES	ALMOST NEVER
1.	Do you feel nervous or depressed (very sad)?	0	1	2
2.	Can you relax easily?	2	1	0
3.	Are you worried about the future?	0	1	2
4.	Do you have close friends you can talk to about personal matters?	2	1	0
5.	Are you active in any organizations or clubs or do you have hobbies?	2	1	0

Your Total Score _____

NUTRITION		FRE-QUENTLY	SOME-TIMES	ALMOST NEVER
1.	Do you eat different kinds of foods each day (fruits and vegetables; whole grain breads and cereals; lean meats, fish, poultry, and beans; dairy products)?	2	1	0
2.	Do you eat a high-fiber diet: lots of whole-grain breads and cereals, fresh fruits, and fresh vegetables?	2	1	0
3.	Do you try *not* to eat foods that have a lot of saturated fat and cholesterol (fatty red meats, eggs, butter, cream, and organ meats such as liver)?	2	1	0
4.	Do you try *not* to eat salty foods or add salt?	2	1	0
5.	Do you try *not* to eat more than three or four sugary snacks, desserts, or soft drinks each week?	2	1	0

Your Total Score _____

FITNESS

	FRE-QUENTLY	SOME-TIMES	ALMOST NEVER
1. Do you do aerobic exercise (running, swimming, quick walking, bicycling) for fifteen to twenty minutes at least three times a week?	4	2	0
2. How often are you at or near the weight that you should be?	3	1	0
3. Do you have a job or other daily activity that keeps you physically active?	2	1	0
4. Do you do stretching exercises at least three times a week?	1	0	0

Your Total Score _____

Survey Results

How did you do? Go back to each section and find your total score. Write each total score in the spaces below.

Smoking _____

Alcohol and Drugs _____

Stress _____

Nutrition _____

Fitness _____

For each lifestyle factor, if your score is:

10–9 You're taking excellent care of yourself in this area.

8–6 Your lifestyle is pretty healthy, but take a second look at any questions in this area where you scored 0 or 1, and think about how you might raise your score.

5–3 You probably need help changing your lifestyle in that area and need more information to make the correct changes.

2–0 Your health is probably in serious danger. You need to make some big changes. You need to talk with a health or fitness professional.

Compare your scores in groups. Who has the healthiest lifestyle?

Part II   Main Dialogue

Exercise 1

Directions: Listen to the dialogue and try to get a general idea of what is happening. Remember, you don't need to understand everything. Just try to think about the following questions:

- Where do you think the dialogue is taking place?
- How do you think the speakers sound (warm, cold, concerned, angry, and so on)?
- How old do you think the speakers are?
- In your opinion, do the speakers live in the city or in the country?

Exercise 2

rewind

Directions: Now, listen to the dialogue again to answer these questions:

1. Why have Emily, Vicky, and Larry come to the Multiple Organic Diner?
2. Who has been to this restaurant before: Emily, Vicky, or Larry?
3. How are Emily, Vicky, and Larry related?
4. What do you think Emily, Vicky, and Larry look like? Give a brief description of each.
5. According to the dialogue, what is important for good health?
6. How does each speaker feel at the end of the dialogue?

Exercise 3

rewind

Directions: Listen to the dialogue one more time. For each item in the chart, put a check (✓) under the name of the person for whom the item is true; put an (**X**) under the name of the person for whom the item is not true, and put a question mark (**?**) under the name of the person if you cannot tell whether the item is true.

	Emily	Vicky	Larry
Smokes			
Has already stopped smoking			
Needs to lose weight			
Drinks alcohol			
Loves health food			
Loves red meat			
Loves running			
Loves swimming			
Loves handball			
Loves tennis			
Needs to become healthier			

Exercise 4   **Directions:** Listen to the sentences from the dialogue and circle the answer that
has the same meaning.

1. **(a)** I think this restaurant might be dirty and uncomfortable.

    (b) I think this restaurant might be too expensive.

2. **(a)** I thought you wanted to stop smoking.

    (b) I thought you wanted to begin exercising.

3. **(a)** The food is good for you.

    (b) The food is delicious.

4. **(a)** Hamburgers make you feel full.

    (b) Hamburgers are bad for your health.

5. **(a)** I don't want to wear black clothes.

    (b) I don't want to become a widow.

6. **(a)** It has a chocolate flavor.

    (b) It gives you a lot of energy.

Part III   Expansion

Section 1
Diet and Exercise

Exercise 1A   **Directions:** Read the following passage and discuss it with your instructor.

The average North American is overweight. There are many reasons
for this. One major reason is that many Americans don't get enough exercise. In North America, machines do most of the kind of work that people in
other parts of the world must do themselves. Another cause of obesity (being overweight) is that Americans often eat when they are not hungry.
People eat when they are happy, when they are sad, or when they are
lonely or bored. Because of this problem of obesity, North Americans have
become very diet conscious.

Today, North Americans are very interested in diet and exercise. Just
go to any bookstore and you will see shelves filled with books about diet
and exercise. Look through your TV listings and you will see that there are
many shows about these two topics. New diet and exercise programs are
introduced each year, but not all of them work and, more important, not all
of them are safe. If you are interested in starting a diet or exercise program,
first consult your doctor.

Exercise 1B **Directions:** With a partner, study the table Suggested Body Weights to answer the following questions.

1. Is your body weight correct for your height?

2. About how many pounds are included in each range of weights listed in this chart?

3. For a man who is five feet ten inches tall the range is 140 to 174 pounds. Does this mean that any weight between 140 and 174 pounds is good for a five-foot-ten-inch man? If not, why not?

4. The range for a woman who is five feet six inches tall is 114 to 146. What would a good weight be for a five-foot-six-inch woman who has a large build? (Give a weight with a ten-pound range.) For a five-foot-six-inch woman who has a small build? For a five-foot-six-inch woman who has an average build?

5. What do you think is an acceptable weight range for a five-foot man?

6. What do you think is an acceptable weight range for a six-foot-two-inch woman?

Suggested Body Weights		
Range of Acceptable Weight		
Height (feet-inches)	Men (pounds)	Women (pounds)
4'10"		91–119
4'11"		94–122
5'0"		96–125
5'1"		99–128
5'2"	112–141	102–131
5'3"	115–144	105–134
5'4"	118–148	108–138
5'5"	121–152	111–142
5'6"	124–156	114–146
5'7"	128–161	118–150
5'8"	132–166	122–154
5'9"	136–170	126–158
5'10"	140–174	130–163
5'11"	144–179	134–168
6'0"	148–184	138–173
6'1"	152–189	
6'2"	156–194	
6'3"	160–199	
6'4"	164–204	

Note: Height without shoes: weight without clothes.
Source: HEW conference on obesity.

Directions: Look at the table Suggested Body Weights again while you listen to the following questions. Take notes to help you organize the information. Then, circle the correct answer for each question you hear.

1. **(a)** five feet, 96 to 125 pounds

   (b) five feet two inches, 112 to 141 pounds

   (c) six feet two inches, 156 to 194 pounds

2. **(a)** 148 to 184 pounds

   (b) 156 to 184 pounds

   (c) 138 to 173 pounds

3. **(a)** 112 to 141 pounds

   (b) 108 to 138 pounds

   (c) 118 to 148 pounds

4. **(a)** 140 to 174 pounds

   (b) 144 to 179 pounds

   (c) 148 to 184 pounds

5. **(a)** The man

   (b) The woman

6. **(a)** The man

   (b) The woman

Exercise 1D

Directions: Listen to the following descriptions and fill in the correct information you hear for each person. Then decide whether each person is at the correct weight.

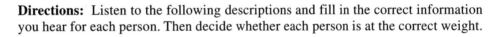

	Sex	Build	Height	Weight
1				
2				
3				
4				
5				
6				

Section 2
Counting Calories

A calorie is a unit used to measure the amount of energy that each kind of food contains. If you take in more calories than the amount of energy your body uses, you gain weight. If you take in fewer calories than the amount of energy your body uses, you lose weight. One pound of weight equals 3,500 calories.

Exercise 2A **Directions:** With a partner study the table Calorie Contents of Selected Foods on the next page to answer the following questions.

1. Look at the Meats and Poultry section. Which food has the fewest calories? Is this food really the lowest in calories? Why or why not?

2. Look at the Fish and Shellfish section. How big is a portion of cod that has 170 calories? How many calories are in a seven-ounce portion of salmon?

3. How many calories are there in two eggs? How many calories are there if you fry the eggs in two pats of butter? How many calories are there in a breakfast of two fried eggs (fried in two pats of butter), two pieces of white toast with two pats of butter, one cup of orange juice, and one cup of coffee with two teaspoons of sugar?

4. If you were very hungry, but didn't want to take in a lot of calories, which dessert or snack food would be your best choice?

5. About how many calories are there in a salad made of four cups of lettuce, one cup of cucumbers, two tomatoes, and three tablespoons of French dressing?

Exercise 2B **Directions:** Look at the table Calorie Contents of Selected Foods to answer the following questions.

1. _____

2. _____

3. _____

4. _____

5. _____

6. _____

7. _____

8. _____

9. _____

10. _____

Calorie Contents of Selected Foods
(Numbers are rough approximations.)

MEATS AND POULTRY (* = 3 ½ OUNCES)

Bacon, 2 slices	95
Chicken*	216
Hamburger*	286
Hot dog*	304
Pork*	373
Steak*	473
Turkey*	263

FISH AND SHELLFISH (* = 3 ½ OUNCES)

Cod*	170
Crab*	93
Fish sticks*	176
Flounder*	79
Salmon*	217
Shrimp* (fried)	225
Tuna* (canned)	197

FRUIT

1 apple	70
1 banana	130
1 cup fruit cocktail	195
1 cup grapes	102
1 orange	60
1 peach	33
1 cup pineapple	75

VEGETABLES

6 spears asparagus	20
1 cup broccoli	50
1 cup carrots	20
½ cup cucumbers	10
2 cups lettuce	15
1 pickle	11
1 potato (baked)	145
1 tomato	25

DAIRY (* = 1 OUNCE)

American cheese*	106
Cottage cheese (½ cup)	117
Monterey jack cheese*	106
Swiss cheese*	107
1 egg	79
1 cup whole milk	157
1 cup low-fat yogurt	120

GRAINS

1 slice white bread	60
1 slice rye bread	55
1 slice whole wheat bread	55
2 crackers	35
1 cup macaroni	155
1 cup oatmeal	150
1 slice pizza	180
1 cup rice	205
1 roll	160

DESSERTS AND SNACKS

1 slice apple pie	330
1 oz. chocolate	151
1 slice chocolate cake	420
1 cookie	110
1 doughnut	135
½ cup peanuts	421
1 cup popcorn	23
10 potato chips	114

BEVERAGES

12 oz. beer	150
1 cup coffee	2
1 oz. liquor	80
1 cup orange juice	120
8 oz. soda	105
1 cup tea	2
3 oz. wine	75

MISCELLANEOUS ITEMS

1 pat butter	36
1 tbsp. honey	64
1 tbsp. jam	55
1 tbsp. ketchup	19
1 tsp. mustard	4
1 tbsp. peanut butter	93
Salad dressing (1 tbsp.)	
Blue cheese	90
French	60
Mayonnaise	110
Thousand Island	75
1 tsp. sugar	18

Exercise 2C

Directions: You will hear five customers ordering food in a restaurant. Circle the letter of the correct order for each customer.

1. _____

(a)	(b)	(c)
½ cup cottage cheese	½ cup fruit cocktail	½ cup of cottage cheese
a sliced tomato	a sliced tomato	a sliced potato
6 spears asparagus	6 spears asparagus	6 spears asparagus
a cup of fresh pineapple	a cup of low-fat yogurt	a cup of fresh pineapple
a cup of black coffee	a cup of black coffee	a cup of black tea

2. _____

(a)	(b)	(c)
salmon	steak, medium rare	steak, blood rare
baked potato	baked potato	baked potato
beer	beer	beer

3. _____

(a)	(b)	(c)
turkey sandwich on toasted whole wheat bread with mayonnaise	turkey sandwich on plain whole wheat bread with mustard	turkey sandwich on toasted whole wheat bread with mustard
iced tea	iced tea	iced tea
2 sugars	2 sugars	2 sugars

4. _____

(a)	(b)	(c)
oatmeal	3 slices pizza	oatmeal
potato salad	beer	banana
2 slices pizza	apple pie	3 slices pizza
beer		beer
		apple pie

5. _____

(a)	(b)	(c)
milk	fish sticks	milk
chocolate cake	milk	cookies
	cookies	

Exercise 2D   Now figure out the total number of calories for each order in exercise 2C.

Customer 1 _____

Customer 2 _____

Customer 3 _____

Customer 4 _____

Customer 5 _____

Which meal is the healthiest? Why?

Section 3

The Environment

Exercise 3A **Directions:** Read the following passage with your instructor and discuss the meaning.

As we have seen, being healthy and fit means taking good care of our bodies and making smart choices. Many people around the world are becoming interested in finding ways to make the earth a healthier and cleaner place to live. We often hear stories in the news about environmental problems such as pollution (dirty air, dirty water, oil spills, litter, and so on), acid rain, and destruction of the rain forests and endangered animals. Many of us wonder what we can do to help save the environment. One way we can all help is to recycle our trash.

Recycling means using old materials such as glass, aluminum, and paper to make new products. When we recycle materials, we throw away less garbage. Recycling also saves energy and natural resources because we don't have to make as many new products.

To help save the environment, it is important to recycle materials and try *not* to buy products in packages that cannot be recycled. Many communities have recycling centers where people can bring materials, and some cities even have curbside recycling to pick up materials at homes. For more information about recycling programs in your community, check your telephone book.

Exercise 3B **Directions:** Listen to the following dialogue and fill in the chart with the correct information.

Recycling service	Days	Location	Time	Item(s)
Curbside recycling				
Recycling center				
Evergreen Society Thrift Store				

Part IV   Focus: Conditionals

You have already studied conditional sentences and know that when you hear an *if* clause, the result can happen when and *only* when the condition (in the *if* clause) occurs. In other words, without the action in the *if* clause, the result cannot occur.

Look at the following sentence:

If I have the money, I will join the health club.

You know that one thing must happen before I can join the health club: I must have the money. You also know that this is a *real conditional sentence* because the verb *have* in the *if* clause is in the simple present tense. Real conditional sentences tell you that the results are possible although they are not certain to happen.

Exercise 1

Directions: Listen to the following real conditional or result clauses and circle the clauses that can be joined to them.

Example   **(a)**   I will join the health club.

           (b)   I will work hard.

1. **(a)** if her doctor tells her to.

   (b) if she loses weight.

2. **(a)** if he loses fifteen more pounds.

   (b) if he looks very handsome.

3. **(a)** you won't be so lazy.

   (b) your fitness will improve.

4. **(a)** if we are healthier.

   (b) if we drive our cars less.

5. **(a)** she will take in too many calories.

   (b) chocolate cake will be her favorite dessert.

Now look at this sentence:

If I had the money, I would join the health club.

You know that this is an *unreal conditional sentence* because the verb *had* in the *if* clause is in the simple past. The simple past in the *if* clause tells you that the result cannot happen because the condition does not really exist. The speaker has no reason to believe that the result can or will happen.

Therefore, I will not join the health club because I do not believe that I will have the money. I can only imagine (dream about) joining the health club.

Unreal conditional sentences make predictions about events based on imaginary conditions. They are useful because they show how the speaker believes events would or could occur if unreal conditions became real.

Exercise 2   **Directions:** Listen to the following unreal conditional or result clauses and circle the clauses that can be joined to them.

Example   **(a)**   I would join the health club.

           (b)   I would work hard.

1.   **(a)** her doctor would tell her to.

      (b) she would lose weight.

2.   **(a)** he would lose fifteen more pounds.

      (b) he would look very handsome.

3.   **(a)** if you weren't so lazy.

      (b) if you improved your fitness.

4.   **(a)** we would be healthier.

      (b) we would drive our cars less.

5.   **(a)** if she took in too many calories.

      (b) if chocolate cake were her favorite.

Review

When you hear a real conditional sentence, which uses the simple present tense, you know that the speaker believes that the result is possible. You do *not* have to understand every word to know that the result is possible.

When you hear an unreal conditional sentence that uses the simple past tense, you know that the speaker believes that the result is not possible. You do *not* have to understand every word to know that the result is not possible.

Your knowledge of real and unreal conditional sentences will help you be a better listener and understand some very important information.

Exercise 3   **Directions:** Listen to the following sentences. Then, circle the correct answer.

     Example   **(a)** I might join a health club.

                  (b) I won't join a health club.

1. **(a)** I might go running with you.

    (b) My knees are not strong.

2. **(a)** We all recycle.

    (b) The environment might improve.

3. **(a)** I live near the park.

    (b) I won't go running every day.

4. **(a)** I might join a health club.

    (b) I won't get in shape.

5. **(a)** We will damage the earth's ozone layer.

    (b) We might damage the earth's ozone layer.

Remember, you don't need to understand every word to understand whether the speaker believes that the result is possible.

Part V   Listening Practice

Exercise 1   **Directions:** You will hear six questions. Read the three possible responses and circle the correct answer.

1. **(a)** I will go on a diet and exercise more.

    (b) I'm not sure. I need to talk to my doctor about that.

    (c) Yes, I want to lose some weight.

2. **(a)** Take them to the recycling center.

    (b) Leave them by the curb in front of your house.

    (c) It will help to save natural resources and energy.

3. **(a)** A hamburger.

    (b) An apple.

    (c) A glass of milk.

4. **(a)** No, I should.

    (b) Yes, I should.

    (c) Yes, I shouldn't.

5. **(a)** I have been jogging for about six months.

    (b) Every Monday, Wednesday, and Friday and every other Sunday.

    (c) I already look and feel much better.

6. **(a)** It's high in cholesterol.

    (b) It's high in fat.

    (c) It's high in vitamins.

Exercise 2   **Directions:** You will hear six sentences. Read the three choices and circle the correct answer.

1. **(a)** I hope you will play tennis with us.

    (b) I know you won't play tennis with us.

    (c) I think you can play tennis with us.

2. **(a)** A hot dog has more calories.

    (b) A turkey sandwich has more calories.

    (c) A hot dog is more nutritious.

3. **(a)** I like my weight.

    (b) I want to lose more weight.

    (c) I have lost fifteen pounds.

4. **(a)** I am going to go swimming every day.

    (b) I might go swimming every day.

    (c) I'm not going to go swimming every day.

5. **(a)** The recycling center is open Saturday night.

    (b) The recycling center is open Wednesday night.

    (c) The recycling center is open Monday afternoon.

6. **(a)** Frances smokes and hates to exercise.

    (b) Dan smokes and hates to exercise.

    (c) They both smoke and hate to exercise.

Exercise 3   **Directions:** Listen to the conversations. Each time you hear the bell, circle the sentence that you think is correct.

Conversation 1

1. (a) The man is being honest.

    (b) The man is being rude.

2. (a) The man is being honest.

    (b) The man is being rude.

Conversation 2

1. (a) The man is ordering a healthy lunch.

    (b) The man is ordering an unhealthy lunch.

2. (a) The man is ordering a healthy lunch.

    (b) The man is ordering an unhealthy lunch.

Exercise 4

Directions: You will hear four conversations. At the beginning of each conversation, you will hear a question. Listen to the conversation. Then, circle the best answer.

1. **(a)** $50.00
    (b) $200.00
    (c) $130.00

2. **(a)** Swimming and dancing
    (b) Dancing and bike riding
    (c) Bike riding and basketball

3. **(a)** Throw them away
    (b) Recycle them
    (c) Save them

4. **(a)** His health and gaining weight
    (b) His family and his health
    (c) Gaining weight and nonsmokers

Part VI   Using It: Making Healthy Changes

Exercise

Directions: Many people today are trying to improve their health and lifestyles. In this exercise, pretend that your friend Maria has come to you for help with the problems described in the following passage. In small groups, create a health program for her. Be sure that the program you create has specific advice for each of her problems. For example, do not simply tell Maria to stop smoking. Instead, suggest exactly what she could do to help her stop (get a nicotine patch, for example).

After your group has created the program, share it with the rest of the class. Then, the class as a whole should decide which group has the best program.

HOW DO YOU SOLVE THE PROBLEMS OF MARIA?

Maria is forty-five years old and is at least thirty pounds overweight. She smokes two packs of cigarettes a day and has a glass of wine with dinner every evening.

Maria works for an insurance company and her schedule is very busy. She drives to work at 6:30 every morning and doesn't return home until after 8:00 at night. The insurance company is having serious financial problems and she is worried that she might be laid off.

Watching old movies on television and talking on the phone are Maria's favorite pastimes. She is also a fantastic baker and loves to make cakes and cookies to share with all of her friends.

Because Maria is so busy, she usually doesn't have time to cook dinner during the week, so she usually eats fast foods or store-bought, frozen dinners.

Last week Maria went for a checkup and her doctor told her that she is worried because Maria has high blood pressure and a high cholesterol level. In addition, Maria has a history of diabetes in her family.

Maria is ready to make changes in her life! What do you suggest?

CHAPTER TEN

Geography and Holidays: "Cruisin' Cross Country"

Part I   Pre-listening

Exercise 1A   **Directions:** Write the full name of the American state or Canadian province next to the abbreviation on Map 1A or B of the United States and Canada on pages 132–33. Refer to the following list of state and province names. The first one, Alabama, has been done for you.

UNITED STATES

Alabama	Kentucky	Ohio
Alaska	Louisiana	Oklahoma
Arizona	Maine	Oregon
Arkansas	Maryland	Pennsylvania
California	Massachusetts	Rhode Island
Colorado	Michigan	South Carolina
Connecticut	Minnesota	South Dakota
Delaware	Mississippi	Tennessee
District of	Missouri	Texas
Columbia (capital)	Montana	Utah
Florida	Nebraska	Vermont
Georgia	Nevada	Virginia
Hawaii	New Hampshire	Washington
Idaho	New Jersey	West Virginia
Illinois	New Mexico	Wisconsin
Indiana	New York	Wyoming
Iowa	North Carolina	
Kansas	North Dakota	

CANADA

Alberta	Newfoundland	Prince Edward Island
British Columbia	Nova Scotia	Québec
Manitoba	Ontario	Saskatchewan
New Brunswick	Ottawa (capital)	

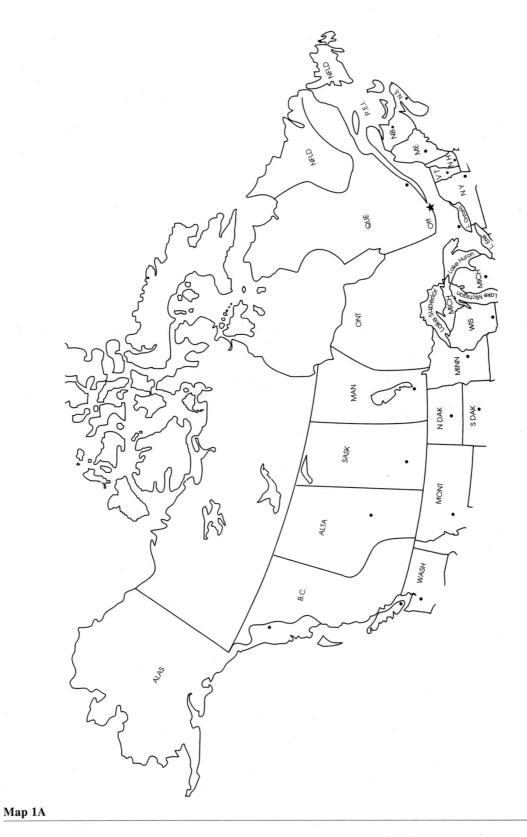

Map 1A

This page is a map of Canada and the states that border it.

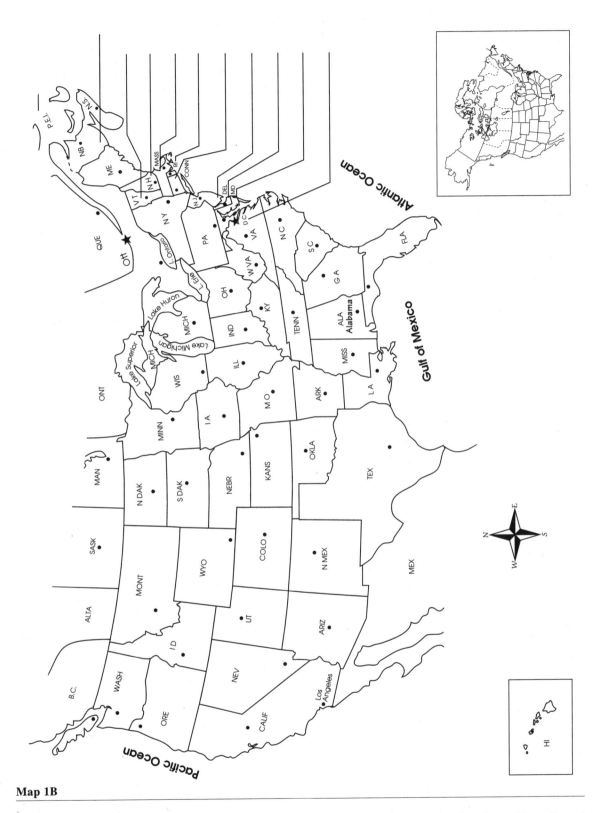

Map 1B

This page is a map of the "lower 48" states, the Canadian provinces that border them, Hawaii, and part of Mexico. The small map in the right-hand corner gives a complete picture of Alaska, Canada, and the lower 48 states together.

Exercise 1B   **Directions:** Look at Map 1A and B again to answer the following questions with a partner.

1. Why does West Virginia have the word *west* in its name?
2. What states and provinces are on the Pacific Coast?
3. How many states and provinces have the word *new* in them? Name them.
4. What states and provinces are on the Atlantic Coast?
5. How many states have the word *north* in them? Name them.
6. What is south of the United States?
7. How many states share a border with Canada? Name them.
8. How many states have the word *south* in them? Name them.
9. Which state is separated from the lower forty-eight states by Canada? Which state isn't located in North America?
10. Find Colorado on your map. If you go from Colorado to Kansas, in which direction are you going? If you go from Colorado to Utah, in which direction are you going? Which state is north of Colorado? Which state is south of Colorado? If you go from Colorado to Nebraska, in which direction are you going? If you go from Colorado to Oklahoma, in which direction are you going?

Part II   Main Dialogue

Exercise 1

Directions: Listen to the dialogue and try to get the general idea of what is happening. Remember, you don't need to understand everything. Just try to think about the following questions:

- Where do you think this dialogue is taking place?
- How old do you think the speakers are?
- What do you think their relationship is?
- Do the speakers sound happy, angry, sad, friendly, unfriendly, sarcastic, annoyed, patient, impatient, and so on?

Exercise 2

rewind

Directions: Go back to the map in Part I. Listen to the dialogue again and draw a line connecting all of the places that Don and Gary plan to visit. Start in L.A. (*Note:* Don't forget to include the states they pass through but don't visit.)

Exercise 3

Directions: Listen to these sentences from the dialogue and circle the answer that has the same meaning.

1. (a) It gets too busy.

   (b) It gets too hot.

2. (a) We can make a quick, one-night stop in Salt Lake City.

   (b) We should be careful about accidents in Salt Lake City.

3. (a) Do we have to spend money on a hotel?

   (b) Do we have to make a hotel reservation?

4. (a) They would go many places with us.

   (b) They would let us stay with them.

5. (a) I want to look at the different styles of the buildings.

   (b) I want to look at the different kinds of people.

6. (a) What's the cost of our trip?

   (b) What's the schedule for our trip?

7. (a) I think you drive fast.

   (b) I think you drive dangerously.

Exercise 4

rewind

Directions: Listen to the dialogue one more time. Then, for each site Don and Gary will visit, fill in the chart with as much information as you can about the state in which each site is located, including the number of days they plan to stay and the activities they might participate in. (Do not worry about spelling.)

	State	No. of days	Accommodations	Activities
Grand Canyon				
Salt Lake City			X	X
Yellowstone National Park				
Mt. Rushmore				
Minneapolis				
Chicago				

Exercise 5   **Directions:** Looking at the map of the United States and Canada from Part I, discuss the following questions with a partner or in small groups.

1. In which states that Gary and Don will go through do they not plan to visit a site?

2. Fill in your city on the map. Then, fill in any other cities that you know.

3. How many states do you go through if you take the shortest route from Florida to California? What are they?

4. How many states and provinces do you go through to go from Newfoundland to Illinois by land? What are they? (Be sure to choose the shortest route.)

5. Choose a place you would like to visit. Draw a line from your state to your destination. What states or provinces do you need to go through to get there?

Part III   Expansion
Section 1
American Regions, Rivers, Mountains, and Lakes

Exercise 1A   **Directions:** Listen to the following descriptions of the regions of the United States and fill in the information on Map 2 according to the instructions you hear.

Exercise 1B   **Directions:** With a partner, fill in Map 2 with the names of the following rivers, mountain ranges, and lakes. Use the clues provided if you need help. Be sure to go in order.

1. *The four longest rivers* (in order according to length):

The Mississippi

The Missouri

The Rio Grande

The Colorado

2. *The two biggest mountain ranges:*

The Rocky Mountains (west of the Mississippi River)

The Appalachian Mountains (east of the Mississippi River)

3. *The five Great Lakes:*

Lake Michigan (the only Great Lake not shared by both the United States and Canada)

Lake Ontario (the smallest Great Lake)

Lake Superior (the largest Great Lake)

Lake Erie (north of Ohio)

Lake Huron (west of Lake Erie and Lake Ontario)

Exercise 1C   **Directions:** Look at Map 2 and listen to the following statements. Decide whether each statement is True or False and circle your answer. (Take notes and refer back to the map if you can't decide right away.)

1. True False	4. True False	7. True False	10. True False
2. True False	5. True False	8. True False	
3. True False	6. True False	9. True False	

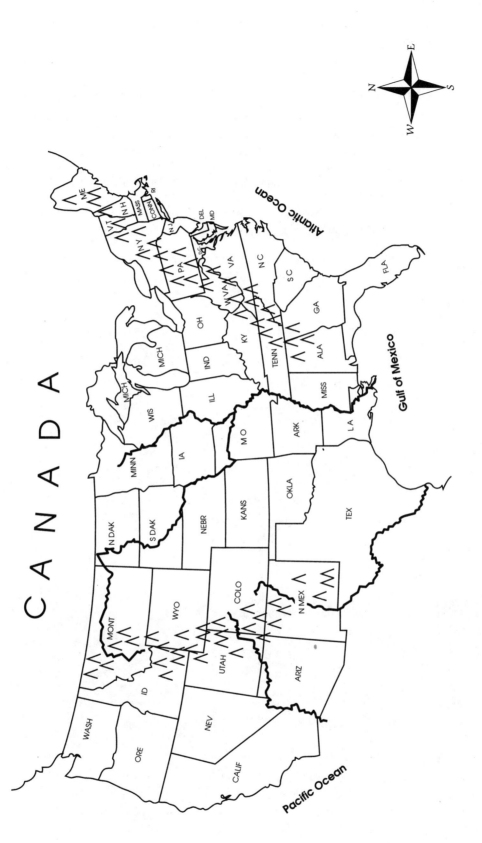

Map 2   The United States

Section 2

American Holidays

Exercise 2A **Directions:** Read and discuss the following information with your instructor.

All countries have holidays. The United States has many holidays that can be described as *religious, national,* or *ethnic* holidays.

Religious holidays celebrate events and include special customs for different religious groups, such as Christians, Jews, Muslims, and so on.

National holidays celebrate important events in the history of the country.

Ethnic holidays celebrate the customs and traditions that were brought to the United States originally from other countries.

Exercise 2B **Directions:** Listen to the following lecture about American holidays. Fill in the chart with the information you hear.

Holiday	Date or time of year	Kind of holiday (circle one)	Things people do to celebrate
Christmas		Religious National Ethnic	
Rosh Hashanah (Jewish New Year)		Religious National Ethnic	
Thanksgiving		Religious National Ethnic	
Independence Day		Religious National Ethnic	
Labor Day		Religious National Ethnic	
St. Patrick's Day		Religious National Ethnic	
Cinco de Mayo		Religious National Ethnic	
Chinese New Year		Religious National Ethnic	

Exercise 2C   **Directions:** In small groups, discuss the following questions:

   1. What holidays not mentioned in the lecture are also celebrated in the United States? For each holiday, list its name, the date or time of the year it occurs, the kind of holiday it is, and the things people do to celebrate it. (Look at a calendar if you need help.)

   2. What holidays celebrated in the United States are also celebrated in your native country? Are the celebrations the same? If not, how are they different?

   3. Describe a holiday from your native country that is not celebrated in the United States.

Exercise 2D   **Directions:** Listen to the following conversations about different holidays. After each conversation, write the number of the conversation next to the correct holiday on the chart in Exercise 2B. Write down any words that helped you figure out the correct answer.

Part IV   Focus: Expressions of Time

To show the time that an action occurs, we use time words or phrases such as *last* month, *the day before yesterday, yesterday, today, now, tomorrow, the day after tomorrow, next* year, *at* six o'clock, *in* the morning, *on* Monday, *in* September, *in* 1965, and so on.

In addition, there are other ways of showing when an action happens without naming the specific hour, day, dates, month or year. With these expressions, we look at a time in relationship to *now*.

Exercise 1 **Directions:** With your teacher, review the following chart below that includes many of these time expressions.

Expression	Time indicated	Examples
In	(Future tense + *in*) Counting time from now until action starts in future	Gary and Don will begin their vacation *IN two weeks.*
Ago	(Simple past tense + *ago*) Counting time back from now until past action occurred	Gary and Don traveled to Mexico *three years AGO.*
For	(Past, Present, or future + *for*) Counting length of any time	The boys stayed in Vancouver *FOR one week.* The boys will stay in Chicago *FOR three nights.*
For Since*	(Present Perfect + *for* or *since*) Counting length of time from beginning of action that began in past and has continued until now	The boys have been planning their trip *FOR one month.* The boys have been planning their trip *SINCE* April.*
Already	(Present Perfect + *already*) Time of action was completed before now	The boys have *ALREADY* visited Mexico.
Yet	(Present Perfect Negative + *yet*) Action has not been completed at any time before now	The boys haven't visited Mt. Rushmore *YET.*
Still	(Present tense + *still*) Action happened in past and also happens now	Don and Gary *STILL* live in Los Angeles.
Anymore	(Negative + *anymore*) Action happened in past, but does not happen now	The boys don't go on vacation with their parents *ANYMORE.*
Within By*	(Future tense + *by* or *within*) Action will be finished before a future time	The boys will return *WITHIN three weeks.* The boys will return *BY September 1.**

*Note that with these two expressions, a specific hour, day, date is necessary.

Your knowledge of these time words can help you understand when an action takes place even if the speaker doesn't mention the specific hour, day, date, month, or year. As with all other structure clues to meaning, it is important to listen for these time expressions to improve your listening comprehension.

Exercise 2

Directions: Look at the calendar. (Note the word *today* is written on the 14th.) Listen to the following statements to figure out the day *or* days indicated in each sentence. Write the dates on the blank lines.

Example **a.** _September 13_____.

b. _Maybe today. Maybe tomorrow. Maybe Monday._____.

1. a. _____

b. _____

2. _____

3. _____

4. a. _____

b. _____

5. _____

6. _____

7. _____

8. _____

SUN.	MON.	TUES.	WED.	THURS.	FRI.	SAT.
1	2 Labor Day	3	4	5	6	7
8 Grandparents Day	9 Rosh Hashanah	10	11	12	13	14 Today
15	16	17 Citizenship Day	18 Yom Kippur	19	20	21
22	23	24	25	26	27	28
29	30					

SEPTEMBER
Flower: Aster / Birthstone: Sapphire

Calendar for September

Exercise 3   **Directions:** Listen to the following sentences. Then, circle the sentence that best follows.

1. (a) The vacation lasted six weeks.

    (b) The vacation lasted two months.

2. (a) It continues to be the largest state.

    (b) It was the largest state before, but not now.

3. (a) They probably want to go there for their vacation.

    (b) They probably want to go somewhere else for their vacation.

4. (a) She can arrive anytime around 9:00 A.M.

    (b) She can arrive anytime before 9:00 A.M.

5. (a) You must wait for that fare.

    (b) You can have that fare anytime during the next three weeks.

6. (a) You must wait for that fare.

    (b) You can have that fare anytime during the next three weeks.

7. (a) He celebrated it before and now.

    (b) He didn't celebrate it before, but does now.

8. (a) You could buy fireworks before, but not now.

    (b) You could never buy fireworks.

9. (a) I need to make plans.

    (b) I don't need to make plans.

10. (a) We'll get there before the end of five days.

    (b) It will take five days to get there.

Part V   Listening Practice

Exercise 1   **Directions:** You will hear seven questions. Read the three possible responses and circle the correct answer.

1. **(a)** October 12.

    (b) National.

    (c) A parade.

2. **(a)** Yes, you certainly can.

    (b) Call a travel agency.

    (c) Go east on Route 40.

3. **(a)** No, I'm worried about him.

    (b) Yes, he'll come back tomorrow.

    (c) Yes, he's still here.

4. **(a)** Because Hawaiians wanted to be able to vote.

    (b) That happened in 1960.

    (c) Yes, it's the fiftieth state in the United States.

5. **(a)** Have barbecues.

    (b) Have parades.

    (c) Go to church.

6. **(a)** Yes, they do.

    (b) Let's look at the map.

    (c) All regions except the northeast.

7. **(a)** Only one.

    (b) Memorial Day.

    (c) Labor Day.

Directions: You will hear six sentences. Read the three choices and circle the correct answer.

1. (a) You could do it before, but not now.

   (b) You could do it before and now.

   (c) You couldn't do it before, but can now.

2. (a) Iowa is north of Wisconsin.

   (b) Iowa is south of Wisconsin.

   (c) Iowa is east of Wisconsin.

3. (a) They made me angry.

   (b) They let me stay with them.

   (c) They didn't tell me what to do.

4. (a) You will be able to camp three months from now.

   (b) You will not be able to camp three months from now.

   (c) You can camp now.

5. (a) I'm going to send a valentine and flowers.

   (b) I'm not going to send a valentine and flowers.

   (c) I'm not sure if I will send a valentine and flowers.

6. (a) He will cross the Mississippi River.

   (b) He will cross the Missouri River.

   (c) He will cross the Colorado River.

Exercise 3

Directions: Listen to the conversation. Each time you hear the bell, circle the sentence that you think is correct.

1. (a) The person can speak French.

   (b) The person can't speak French.

2. (a) The person can speak French.

   (b) The person can't speak French.

3. (a) The person likes Montreal.

   (b) The person doesn't like Montreal.

4. (a) The person likes Montreal

   (b) The person doesn't like Montreal

   (c) We don't know.

Exercise 4

Directions: You will hear three conversations. At the beginning of each conversation, you will hear a question. Listen to the conversation. Then, circle the best answer.

1. (a) The Pacific Coast states

    (b) The Southern states

    (c) The Northeastern states

2. (a) Christmas

    (b) Thanksgiving

    (c) St. Patrick's Day

3. (a) The Midwest

    (b) New England

    (c) The Southwest

Part VI   Using it: Travel and Holiday Fun

Exercise

Directions: With a partner choose one of the following activities. After you have finished working on your activity, share your work with the rest of the class.

Activity 1: Choose a location in the United States or Canada to describe to the class. Without giving the name of the location, say what region of the country it is located in. Describe which states or provinces are near your location (use expressions such as *north of, south of, southeast of,* and so on). Also, remember to add information about mountains, rivers, culture and economy of the region, and anything else that is important. When you finish your description, ask the class to guess your location.

Activity 2: Plan a road trip to a location at least several days away from your home. Answer the following questions for the class:

1. How long will your trip take?
2. What will your itinerary be?
3. How much money do you think you will need?
4. Which sites will you visit along the way?
5. Where will you sleep in each city or town that you visit?

Use a map to point out each place that you discuss.

Activity 3: Choose an American holiday and plan a celebration for that day. Answer the following questions for the class:

1. When will the celebration take place? (date and time)
2. What kinds of clothing will people need to wear?
3. What kinds of food will you serve?
4. What kinds of activities will you plan?
5. What kinds of decorations will you need?

Add any other information that you can think of.

Activity 4: Plan a celebration for a new holiday called ESL Students' Day. Answer the following questions for the class:

1. What is the reason for this holiday?
2. When does this holiday take place?
3. What kinds of activities take place on this holiday?
4. What kinds of food are served?
5. Are gifts exchanged? If yes, who gives gifts to whom? Add any other information that you can think of.